In this gripping – and timely – account Brian Bailey looks at the history of human imprisonment from the earliest times to the present day. From the stews of Newgate to the supposedly escape-proof Alcatraz and the privatised jails of 90s England, Bailey examines imprisonment, whether for perpetrators of violence or prisoners of conscience. The result is a fascinating study of the arguments for and against the jailing of prisoners and the changes history has made to punishment by imprisonment.

Brian Bailey was born and brought up in Leicestershire and spent most of his early working life in printing and publishing. He became a professional author in the 1970s and has well over a dozen non-fiction titles to his credit. He is married to a photographer and now lives in Devon.

Also by Brian Bailey

Massacres
Hangmen of England
The Assassination File
The Resurrection Men

HELLHOLES
AN ACCOUNT OF HISTORY'S MOST NOTORIOUS PRISONS

Brian Bailey

ORION

An Orion paperback
First published in Great Britain in 1995 by Orion,
an imprint of Orion Books Ltd,
Orion House, 5 Upper St Martin's Lane, London WC2H 9EA

A CIP catalogue record for this book is available
from the British Library

ISBN: 1 85797 669 X

Typeset at Deltatype Limited, Ellesmere Port, Cheshire
Printed and bound in Great Britain by
Clays Ltd, St Ives plc

Contents

But that I am forbid
To tell the secrets of my prison-house,
I could a tale unfold whose lightest word
Would harrow up thy soul, freeze thy young blood,
Make thy two eyes, like stars, start from their spheres,
Thy knotted and combined locks to part,
And each particular hair to stand on end,
Like quills upon the fretful porpentine . . .

William Shakespeare, *Hamlet*

PREFACE

Every society that builds a prison thereby confesses its failure, and even as I write, the British Home Secretary, Michael Howard, announces that six more are to be built in this country. It has been well said that each society gets the criminals it deserves, and the best that can be said of any prison, however humane its government and up-to-date its facilities, is that it is a necessary evil.

Prisons have been much in the news in recent years, with prison riots; British treatment of prisoners in Northern Ireland called into question at the European Court of Human Rights; and a seemingly endless procession of released prisoners whose convictions have been overturned.

Yet our prisons now are models of civilised decency when compared with the treatment prisoners could expect to receive in them in the past, whether in Britain or abroad. This book is an account of how prisons have been run in various countries, in both the distant and the more recent past, and it is a sobering thought that the British influence in this respect has been incalculably high. Some of the prisons I have included are, regrettably, still in business.

In telling the stories of some of mankind's most shameful hellholes, and of the prisoners who have suffered in them, I hope the book will serve as a timely reminder of those abuses of human rights which must be eliminated from our way of life if we are ever to realise the highest ideals of civilisation. This necessity has nothing to do with sympathy for criminals, but everything to do with the well-being of society as a whole. For if society inflicts violence on its criminals, and deals with them cruelly, it irresponsibly reduces itself to the level of those it condemns. As Sir William Blackstone wisely wrote, more than two centuries ago: 'Though the end of punishment is to deter men from offending, it never can follow from thence, that it is lawful to deter them at any rate, and by any means.'

Part 1
BRITAIN'S CRIMINAL PRISONS

INTRODUCTION

Daniel Defoe, recording his impressions of Britain in the 1720s, remarked that there were in London, 'notwithstanding we are a nation of liberty, more public and private prisons, and houses of confinement, than any city in Europe, perhaps as many as in all the capital cities of Europe put together . . .'

Five of the London prisons which existed at that time are dealt with in this book. But it was not only in the capital that gaols proliferated, and from one end of the kingdom to the other they were places of which a nation calling itself civilised ought to have been thoroughly ashamed.

Half a century after Defoe, John Howard travelled the length and breadth of England and Wales considering the state of the prisons, and discovered horrors everywhere he went. Women in Middlesex prisons in 1776 were kept 'almost naked, with only a few filthy rags almost alive with vermin, their bodies rotting with distemper, and covered with itch, scorbutic and venereal ulcers'. At St Albans, Howard found a girl, sentenced to a year's imprisonment, 'locked up all the day with two soldiers in the workroom'. At Oxford, he found the men's quarters swarming with vermin. At Abingdon, petty offenders were kept in irons. At Marlborough, he found a man dying on the bare floor. At Salisbury, debtors were padlocked by their legs to chains at the prison gate. At Swansea, the 'room for felons (called the Black Hole) has an aperture in the door, but no window: yet at the Michaelmas quarter sessions, prisoners of both sexes are here confined for some days'. At Liverpool, 'all the men were in heavy irons, and seven out of eight women were chained to the floors...' At Knaresborough, an open sewer ran through the prison's one room. 'I was informed that an officer, confined here some years since, for only a few days, took in with him a dog to defend him from vermin; but the dog was soon destroyed, and the prisoner's face much disfigured by them'.

Gaol fever was rife almost everywhere. In 1730, a hundred people had died at Taunton when prisoners were brought from the gaol for trial at the assizes. Many people died in Launceston and the surrounding country when prisoners were brought out of prison for the same reason. The notorious case at Newgate in 1750 was only the worst of many serious outbreaks, such as at Gloucester in 1782, when three times as many prisoners died of gaol fever as were executed during the year.

The exposure of prison conditions by humanitarians such as Howard, Elizabeth Fry and Sir Francis Burdett, and the theorising of Jeremy Bentham and others, combined to effect drastic reforms of prisons around the middle of the nineteenth century, but the horror of prison life, alas, did not end there.

More than two and a half centuries after Defoe, the number of people in Britain's prisons was higher, in terms of the ratio of prisoners to total population, than in any country in Europe except for Luxembourg. In late 1988, the British figure was 97.4 per 100,000 of the population. In Germany the figure was 84.9; in Sweden 56; in the Netherlands 48.4. In November of that year the British Home Secretary said that 'we want to make out of date the notion that the only punishment that works is behind bars'. He admitted, though, that it would be a long haul. In the meantime, however up-to-date and humane the standards of modern British prisons may be by comparison with those of the past, or with some modern prisons in other countries, they are still hellholes to many prisoners, as is shown by the number of suicides which occur in them.

NEWGATE PRISON, LONDON

Newgate was the principal common gaol of the capital for more than five hundred years, and as such it became the shame of England. It stood at the western entrance to the City of London, at the junction of Newgate Street and Old Bailey, and was originally part of the gatehouse of one of the oldest city gates, being first mentioned as a prison during the reign of King John. It was thus much senior to the Bastille in Paris, and it has been said that prisoners of rank were committed to it long before the Tower of London came into use as a regular state prison, though that must remain open to some doubt.

Newgate had been badly damaged in the Peasants' Revolt of 1381, when Wat Tyler and his followers had broken in and freed the prisoners; and it was probably in a ruinous condition from that time until Sir Richard Whittington's executors rebuilt it after his death in 1423, Whittington having left money in his will for the new prison. This served for two hundred years – a place regularly overcrowded with prisoners heavily fettered; inadequately fed; denied light and air; swindled by the corrupt keeper and his turnkeys; and if they were not sent to their deaths by rope at Tyburn or flame at Smithfield, dying, as often as not, of gaol fever in their miserable cells, whether they were in for murder, or theft, or debt.

The martyrologist John Foxe referred to many victims of the religious persecutions of the fifteenth and sixteenth centuries being committed to Newgate, before most of them were carted off to Smithfield to be burnt at the stake. But for some, Newgate itself was their life's terminus. Thus William Andrew, a carpenter from Horsley, Essex, was committed on 1 April 1555, and through 'strait handling in the prison, there lost his life'. Jesuits and puritans, horse-thieves and highwaymen, forgers and coiners, rapists and prostitutes; all were thrown indiscriminately into this loathsome place, where they mixed with raving lunatics and infants born to their mothers in the gaol, amid drunkenness, fever, incontinence and smallpox.

There were nearly three hundred prisoners in Newgate in 1642, but during the Great Fire in 1666, the prison was destroyed, or at least seriously damaged. It was rebuilt in the following year, when it was described as the county gaol for Middlesex, for debtors and malefactors, and the city prison for criminals. Most prisoners arriving at Newgate were clapped in irons in the gatehouse until they had paid two shillings and sixpence – a fee known as 'garnish' – whereupon they were admitted to the inner wards. Some criminals were branded on their thumbs with red-hot irons, to mark them forever as thieves or vagabonds, or to show that they had escaped sentence once by claiming benefit of clergy, and could not do so a second time.

There was more than a little irony in the fact that figures of Truth, Justice and Mercy were placed in niches over the main entrance. That prisoners had often suffered ill-treatment in dark and filthy dungeons in the medieval period is not particularly surprising. What made Newgate a place of infamy was that its conditions were hardly ever improved to keep up with the times. Its buildings rose in a squalid maze of damp passages and yards and dark staircases. There were four floors, a cellar and an exercise yard in the new prison. The cellar was partly occupied by the drinking room, where the keeper traditionally made a profit from the sale of beer and liquor.

On the second floor was a room popularly known as

'Jack Ketch's Kitchen', because it was used by the common hangman to boil the quarters of those he had executed for treason. The Quaker Thomas Ellwood, committed to Newgate in the 1660s, left us an account of what happened there:

> When we first came into Newgate, there lay (in a little by-place like a closet, near the room where we were lodged) the quartered bodies of three men, who had been executed some days before, for a real or pretended plot; ... the relatives were all that while petitioning to have leave to bury them; which, at length, with much ado, was obtained for the quarters, but not for the heads, which were ordered to be set up in some part of the City. I saw the heads when they were brought up to be boiled; the hangman fetched them in a dirty dust basket, out of some by-place; and setting them down among the felons, he and they made sport with them. They took them by the hair, flouting, jeering, and laughing at them; and then, giving them some ill names, boxed them on the ears and cheeks. Which done, the Hangman put them into his kettle, and parboiled them with Bay-Salt and Cummin-seed – that to keep them from putrefaction, and this to keep off the fowls from seizing on them.

Close by was the Press Room, where prisoners who refused to plead were subjected to the *peine forte et dure*, or pressing to death. Stretched out on the floor and tightly bound, they had heavy weights of stone or iron piled on their chests until they either submitted or expired, a process sometimes taking several days.

Titus Oates was incarcerated here by Judge Jeffreys in 1678, sentenced to life imprisonment after his merciless flogging from Aldgate to Newgate, and then two days later from the prison to Tyburn, during which he was said to have received upwards of two thousand lashes, though the first flogging was sufficient to render him more or less insensible to the second. 'Ironed in the darkest hole of Newgate', in Macaulay's words, Oates was taken out once a year and exposed on the pillory in different parts of London, and at the mercy of the mob.

It was alleged that in 1718, when the former hangman John Price was awaiting execution for murder, a little girl 'who used to convey victuals' to him in Newgate had declared that 'a few days before his execution, he had carnal knowledge of her body . . .'

Undoubtedly the most celebrated inmate around this period was Jack Sheppard, the young and diminutive housebreaker and expert locksmith who twice escaped from Newgate, despite – on the second occasion – being chained and handcuffed in a gloomy dungeon where he was awaiting execution. It is said that he had to negotiate, without alerting the turnkeys, six iron doors that were all locked and bolted. Nevertheless, Sheppard got his comeuppance at Tyburn in November 1724, aged twenty-two, and that arch-villain and master-thief Jonathan Wild, who had carried on his business from inside the prison as if he were still at home, was also carted off to Tyburn in the following year.

John Howard was told in later years that condemned malefactors who had 'affected an air of boldness during their trial, and appeared quite unconcerned at the pronouncing sentence upon them, were struck with horror, and shed tears, when brought to these darksome solitary abodes'. Common felons who could not pay a fee for a better place were kept in a dark, cold and stinking ward where they had to lie on the stone floor, having no beds. Little wonder that 'gaol fever', the disease since identified as a virulent form of typhus, flourished there. It was described as a 'contagious, putrid, and very pestilential fever, attended with tremblings, twitchings, restlessness, delirium, with, in some instances, early phrenzy and lethargy; while the victims broke out often into livid pustules and purple spots'. An outbreak in 1750 was so infectious that when some prisoners were brought from Newgate for trial, the Lord Mayor of London, two judges, an alderman, two or three counsel, and several jurymen all died from it. The prison was cleaned out and three cartloads of 'the most abominable filth' were removed and buried ten feet deep.

Two years later a windmill was mounted on the gaol roof to draw a draught of air through ventilating shafts, and this produced some slight improvement, but not before workmen installing the equipment had been seriously affected by the foul and loathsome air which produced nausea, headaches and, in at least one case, delirium. The workmen then passed their illnesses on to their wives and children when they went home. Nor did the new device solve the problem entirely. The keeper, Mr Akerman, reported to a Commons committee, some years later, that between 1758 and 1765 eighty-three people had died in Newgate, as well as several women who had visited their husbands in prison, and a number of children who had been born there, and the majority of these fatalities were put down to gaol fever.

Eventually, Parliament commanded the Corporation of the City of London to provide a new building. The first stone was laid in 1770, but progress was tardy. Designed by George Dance the Younger, in a severe classical style, the rebuilt Newgate was not finished until 1778. By this time, John Wilkes, the Sheriff of London, had ordered the keeper to release prisoners from their chains when they were taken to court, for no man in England, he said, 'ought to be obliged to plead while in chains'. Two years after its completion, the new prison was virtually destroyed again in the Gordon Riots. Three hundred prisoners were set free, including three who had been destined for Tyburn the next morning. The poet George Crabbe described what he saw in Old Bailey on the night of 8 June 1780:

The prison was . . . a remarkably strong building; but,

determined to force it, they broke the gates with crows and other instruments, and climbed up the outside of the cell part, which joins the two great wings of the building, where the felons were confined; and I stood where I plainly saw their operations. They broke off the roof, tore away the rafters, and having got ladders they descended. Not Orpheus himself had more courage or better luck; flames all around them, and a body of soldiers expected, they defied and laughed at all opposition.

The prisoners escaped. I stood and saw about twelve women and eight men ascend from their confinement to the open air, and they were conducted through the streets in their chains. Three of these were to be hanged on Friday. You have no conception of the phrensy of the multitude. This being done, and Akerman's house now a mere shell of brickwork, they kept a store of flame there for other purposes. It became red-hot, and the doors and windows appeared like the entrance to so many volcanoes. With some difficulty they then fired the debtors' prison – broke the doors – and they, too, all made their escape.

Tired of the scene, I went home, and returned again at eleven o'clock at night. I met large bodies of horse and foot soldiers coming to guard the Bank, and some houses of Roman Catholics near it. Newgate was at this time open to all; anyone might get in, and, what was never the case before, anyone might get out.

Mr Akerman, whose house had been burnt down by the mob, was a man with such a reputation for humane consideration of his charges that he earned the praise of Samuel Johnson and Edmund Burke, among others. But he could not alter the odious character of the place, and when Casanova was held briefly in the prison, he thought he had come to one of the lowest circles of Dante's *Inferno*.

The prison was thoroughly repaired at a cost of at least twenty thousand pounds. The new Newgate was a forbidding building of granite, with a long rusticated façade. Round the tops of the high walls were *chevaux-de-frise* – horizontal iron bars with revolving iron spikes along them – making it almost impossible for anyone to get over the walls. The prison was divided into separate wards for different categories of prisoners, such as male and female felons, male and female debtors, and there were fifteen condemned cells adjacent to the press yard. There was the usual 'common' side, as opposed to the 'master' side which housed the privileged who could afford to pay the keeper for better accommodation. Guards with firearms and accompanied by dogs watched over the prison throughout the night. The wards were overcrowded and filthy.

When John Howard visited it in 1788, finding six hundred and thirteen prisoners there, he correctly predicted that 'without more than ordinary care, the prisoners in it will be in great danger of the gaol-fever'. Lord George Gordon, leader of the anti-Catholic riots, was arrested and committed to the Tower of London, and accused of treason, but was acquitted on being judged insane. He continued to provoke the authorities, however, and eventually died in Newgate – of gaol fever – in 1793. In 1803, an epidemic of gaol fever accounted for seventy-nine lives in the prison. 'In three or four rooms', Howard had observed,

> there were near a hundred and fifty women crowded together, many young creatures with the old and hardened, some of whom had been confined upwards of two years: on the men's side likewise there were many boys of twelve or fourteen years of age; some almost naked. In the men's infirmary, there were only seven iron bedsteads; and at my last visit, there being twenty sick, some of them, naked and with sores, in a miserable condition, lay on the floor with only a rug. There were four sick in the infirmary for women, which is only fifteen feet and a half by twelve, has but one window, and no bedsteads; sewers offensive: prison not whitewashed.

An Act of 1751 had banned the sale of spirits inside prisons, but the law was generally ignored, and was unenforceable. The Ordinary of Newgate – the prison chaplain – informed Jeremy Bentham in 1783 that women smuggled spirits in 'in such ways that it would be termed the grossest insult to search for them'.

Towards the end of the century, a book of criminal exploits entitled *The Malefactor's Register, or New Newgate and Tyburn Calendar* was published in London, and this became the basis of many subsequent versions of that ever-popular collection of fact and fiction to which the prison gave its name – the *Newgate Calendar*.

Those in Newgate's condemned cells had to endure the dire warnings of the Ordinary, who customarily filled their already troubled minds with apprehensions that, unless they were thoroughly repentant, they were headed for a place where, as Fielding put it, they would be ready to give more for a drop of water than they had ever given for a bottle of wine. A condemned highwayman, Paul Lewis, was so infuriated by the Ordinary in 1763 that he tried to kill him. The Revd Horace Cotton was reprimanded by the authorities in 1824 for delivering a sermon so powerful that it was unnecessarily harrowing to the prisoner about to die.

For hundreds of years, Newgate was the main depot or clearing-house from which condemned prisoners were driven to the human slaughter-house at Tyburn, to be hanged, burnt or butchered by ignorant executioners, at the order of ignorant judges, on behalf of the ignorant populace. For a long period, there were eight 'hanging days' a year at Tyburn. They were public holidays, commonly known as 'Paddington Fair'. Noisy crowds lined the streets as the condemned left Newgate in open horse-drawn carts or hurdles, to the tolling of St Sepulchre's bell, to be drawn the two miles across London. What began as a solemn procession, with the

Ordinary of Newgate accompanying the condemned and exhorting them to confess their sins and make their peace with God, rapidly degenerated into a rowdy shambles, with the excited mob yelling and shoving for a better view, and throwing missiles at the villains if they were especially reviled, or at the hangman if there was some sympathy for the condemned. Almost everyone, including the criminal and the hangman, would usually be under the influence of strong drink.

In 1783 the authorities at last put an end to this periodic exhibition of animal instincts, but only because the Tyburn gallows were becoming an inconvenience to the growing traffic and an embarrassment to the residents of that part of the capital that was to become known as the smart West End. Henceforth, executions would take place in front of Newgate Gaol itself, in Old Bailey. The new scaffold was a mobile structure, which was kept in the prison yard and wheeled out, pulled by horses, on hanging days. On 9 December 1783, ten people were hanged on it at once.

There was an accident with this scaffold in 1797, when two men, Martin Clench and James Mackley, were being prepared on the gallows by the executioner, Brunskill, and his assistant, Langley. The Ordinary, the Revd John Villette, and a Catholic priest were administering the last rites to the two criminals when the platform suddenly collapsed, and all six men fell in a heap. The two clergymen were very shaken and badly bruised. The criminals were said after their execution to be innocent of the murder for which they had been condemned.

This was the period when the corpses of executed murderers were customarily hung in chains on gibbets or handed over to the surgeons for dissection, but when the five leaders of the Cato Street Conspiracy were hanged in front of Newgate in 1820, the sentence was that, as traitors, they should also be beheaded. After their bodies had been left hanging on the gallows for half an hour, a masked figure in a seaman's jersey speedily decapitated them with an axe, and the hangman, James Botting, held up each severed head in turn to the huge crowd.

There was no limit to the number of prisoners committed for debt to Newgate – known to the London underworld as 'the stone jug' – and no limit to the number allowed in to visit them during daylight hours. Hundreds of women and children crowded in and spent their time with the prisoners in revelry and drunkenness, fighting and gambling, indecency and foul language. For a fee of a shilling, any prostitute, who might or might not care to claim she was the wife of a prisoner, was allowed to spend the night in the prison, the female prisoners were similarly allowed to entertain men who only had to say they were their husbands to be allowed in. Women condemned to death were kept in a ward where the chief preoccupation was enticing men – prisoners, visitors, turnkeys or whoever – to copulate with them. Proof of pregnancy – 'pleading the belly' – was the surest way of getting a reprieve.

When Elizabeth Fry first visited Newgate, a quarter of a century after Howard, she found 'disorderly, dram-drinking, half-naked women, vagrants and felons, con-victed and unconvicted alike, some with little children clinging to their skirts, penned up promiscuously in crowded wards and yards, reeking with filth and infested with vermin'.

At this time Newgate, calculated to accommodate four hundred and twenty-seven prisoners, sometimes held as many as twelve hundred. It was said that the keeper was never informed of any prisoner with an illness, however serious, until he got warning to arrange a funeral.

In 1817 Mrs Fry visited a woman prisoner sentenced to death for robbery:

I have just returned from a most melancholy visit to

Newgate, where I have been at the request of Elizabeth Fricker, previous to her execution tomorrow morning, at eight o'clock. I found her much hurried, distressed, and tormented in mind. Her hands cold, and covered with something like the perspiration preceding death, and in an universal tremor. The women who were with her said she had been so outrageous before our going that they thought a man must be sent for to manage her . . . Besides this poor young woman, there are also six men to be hanged, one of whom has a wife near her confinement, also condemned, and seven young children. Since the awful report came down, he has become quite mad, from horror of mind. A strait waistcoat could not keep him within bounds: he had just bitten the turnkey; I saw the man come out with his hand bleeding, as I passed the cell.

Large numbers of convicts were by this time being sentenced to transportation to Australia, and Newgate served as a transit camp for prisoners sent from all parts of Britain to the hulks and the Channel ports of embarkation. One witness saw female prisoners arriving from Lancaster Castle, handcuffed and with heavy irons on their swollen legs. Others were chained together, and had iron hoops round their legs and arms.

A woman brought to Newgate from Carlisle had been deprived of her newborn baby whilst in prison in the north, and the child had been deposited in the parish poor-house, where it would probably perish: '. . . in this state of bodily pain and mental distraction she was brought to Newgate . . . and was then sent out to Botany Bay'. Women prisoners frequently rioted at Newgate before their departure on the next stage of their awful journeys.

The caricaturist George Cruikshank recorded that he was 'returning home between 8 and 9 a.m. down Ludgate Hill, and saw several human beings hanging opposite Newgate, and to my horror two of them were women'. He found on enquiry that they had been hanged for passing forged banknotes. Around this time, William Calcraft, a cobbler who had a profitable sideline selling meat pies among the vast crowds that habitually crushed in and around Old Bailey to witness the executions, got the regular job of flogging juvenile offenders at Newgate, and eventually became the longest-serving executioner known to English history, carrying out hangings both outside and inside the gaol, as well as at other places both in London and the provinces, for forty-five years.

As a journalist, Charles Dickens had been given a two-hour tour of Newgate, and his account in *Oliver Twist* of Fagin in the condemned cell had already been published when, in July 1840, he saw an execution take place there, and later described the crowd milling around outside the prison on these occasions:

> I did not see one token in all the immense crowd; at the windows, in the streets, on the house-tops, anywhere; of any one emotion suitable to the occasion. No sorrow, no salutary terror, no abhorrence, no seriousness; nothing but ribaldry, debauchery, levity, drunkenness, and flaunting vice in fifty other shapes. I should have deemed it impossible that I could have ever felt any large assemblage of my fellow-creatures to be so odious . . .

Despite the criticisms and campaigns of Elizabeth Fry and other reformers, the Corporation of the City of London remained apathetic about conditions in Newgate, and a leading alderman, Sir Peter Laurie, delivered himself of the opinion in 1835 that the prison could not be improved. But a House of Lords Committee had enough common sense to see that imprisonment in Newgate 'must have the effect of corrupting the morals' of the inmates, and tend rather towards the extension of crime than to its suppression. John Howard had said, echoing other similar opinions, that half the crimes committed in and around London were planned inside

Newgate. Edward Gibbon Wakefield, who had spent some time as an inmate himself, had also described the prison as the greatest nursery of crime. Colonel Joshua Jebb told a Select Committee on prison discipline in 1850 that it was one of the worst prisons in England, and W. Hepworth Dixon wrote, in the same year, that Newgate was one of the worst 'hot-beds of vice and moral disease in London'. He drew attention to the case of a sixteen-year-old servant girl who was charged with stealing a brooch and committed to Newgate to await trial. She spent her time there among the 'most abandoned of her sex' day and night, and there was 'no form of wickedness, no aspect of vice' with which she did not become familiar. When her trial finally came, the evidence was found to be so feeble that she was acquitted at once. 'That she entered Newgate innocent, I have no doubt; but who shall answer for the state in which she left it?'

Nevertheless, Newgate remained untouched by progressive theories of penology until the later part of the nineteenth century. True, drinking and gaming in the prison had been abolished, but prisoners still spent up to fifteen hours a day in dark, unheated cells, and some were put to picking oakum during the daytime. Recommendations had been made as long ago as 1830 for the reconstruction of Newgate in keeping with modern ideas, but the Corporation was no more enthusiastic about spending money on rebuilding than it had been about incurring the expense of central heating.

Between 1857 and 1862, at least half a century too late, Newgate was at last extensively modernised, and new cell blocks conforming to the latest 'separate system' were built for both male and female prisoners. Even so, Mayhew found that in 1860 Newgate's prisoners included fifty-two males and eleven females under sixteen years of age. Meanwhile, Pentonville had been completed in 1842, and Holloway in 1851 – two new prisons built on modern principles north of the Thames, with Wandsworth south of the river; and these put Newgate out of the reckoning as a suitable gaol for London in the latter part of the century. It was relegated mainly to a place of detention for those awaiting trial, and its population was accordingly reduced.

In 1868, executions in public were finally abolished by the Capital Punishment Amendment Act. Henceforth, the death penalty was to be administered behind closed doors, and communicated to the outside world by hoisting a black flag on the roof. An execution shed was built in the exercise yard, close to the condemned cells which had been incorporated in the new cell block, and the attic where executioners lodged when engaged there. This was virtually the last structural addition to Newgate prison.

This move was soon followed by the introduction by Calcraft's successor, William Marwood, of the 'long drop'. Centuries of slow strangulation at the ends of ropes were replaced (in most cases, at least, for there were always miscalculations) by the more-or-less instantaneous death resulting from fracture of the cervical vertebrae. Slow strangulation remained the usual cause of death, however, for those driven to suicide, when despairing prisoners hanged themselves with rope, sheets, boot-laces or strips torn from their shirts.

In 1877, the Prisons Act brought all British prisons under the direct control of the state, and it was soon decided that Newgate was redundant. In 1880, it was closed except as a place of temporary confinement for those required to be available during the Old Bailey sessions.

Newgate's execution shed continued to be used for executions in London. The last hangman to be trained at the prison was Henry Pierrepoint, and the last execution there was that of George Woolfe, who was hanged for murder by William and John Billington on 7 May 1902.

The Newgate gallows were removed to Pentonville, where the hallowed English tradition of hanging men by the neck until dead was to continue for another sixty-two years. In 1902, after standing in one form or another for at least seven centuries, Newgate was finally demolished – despite a public outcry against the removal of this ancient symbol of barbarism – to make way for the new Central Criminal Court, which retained part of the old prison's outer wall.

2

THE DEBTORS' PRISONS
IN LONDON

By the eighteenth century, three types of prison were recognised in England. There were secure jails for serious criminals; the houses of correction, or 'bridewells', where people classified as rogues and vagabonds were put to compulsory labour; and the debtors' prisons. A commentator in 1716 reckoned that there were 'about 60,000 miserable debtors perishing in the prisons of England and Wales'. One modern historian of eighteenth-century crime and punishment has written that in the provinces there were 'no separate gaols for debtors', but I have seen beneath Shrewsbury's Music Hall, in the Square, a narrow passage flanked by dark, cramped cells where once, I believe, the town's miserable debtors were incarcerated, and John Howard referred specifically to the prison at Knaresborough, for instance, as a debtors' prison. The most notorious debtors' prisons, however, were the Fleet, the Marshalsea, and the King's Bench, all in London.

The debtors' prisons were a national scandal throughout the century, despite a Parliamentary enquiry in 1728 which mitigated some of the worst abuses. A keeper of the Fleet, Thomas Bainbridge, was dismissed as a result of this enquiry, for treating prisoners in 'the most barbarous and cruel manner'. Nevertheless, keepers and turnkeys maltreated poor prisoners to extort from them money, which, if they had possessed any, would have kept them out of those hellholes in the first place. This evil system was a result of farming out the prisons to unscrupulous wardens in order to avoid the expense to the owners of employing regular salaried staff.

The Fleet Prison, rebuilt after the Great Fire, had existed since the twelfth century, and had already been extensively damaged once before, during the Peasants' Revolt of 1381, when the men of Kent under Wat Tyler 'broke open the prison of the Fleet and turned out all the prisoners, and let them go whither they would . . .'. The prison stood on the east side of Fleet Market, where the modern Farringdon Street follows the course of the underground Fleet River towards the Thames at Blackfriars Bridge. The prison's former site is partly occupied by Caroone House, between Holborn Viaduct and Ludgate Circus. It was once used as a royal prison and those condemned by Star Chamber were sent there. The Fleet became a debtors' prison on the abolition of Star Chamber during the reign of Charles I.

All three of the London debtors' prisons are mentioned in the famous fifteenth-century correspondence of the Paston family, and John Paston was himself confined twice in the Fleet for short periods in 1461 and 1464. Bishop John Hooper was imprisoned there by Mary Tudor in September 1553, and detained for seven months. The warden, one Babington, used him 'very extremely', picking quarrels with him to make an excuse to move him from the quarters for privileged prisoners to close confinement in a 'vile and stinking' room in the Tower chamber. On one side of it ran the prison's own filthy refuse, and on the other the common sewer of the city. The stench and foulness of the place made him sick, as he lay moaning in his own filth. At the end of January 1555, Bishop Hooper was brought out and taken to Gloucester, where he was burned alive at the stake on 9 February.

The Marshalsea was also one of the old London prisons which had been there at least as early as the fourteenth century. It, too, had been burned down during the Peasants' Revolt. The mob hunted down the warden, John Imworth, notorious as a 'pitiless tormen-tor', and when they found him hiding in Westminster Abbey, carried him off to Cheapside where he was promptly beheaded. The odious and sadistic Bishop of London under Bloody Mary, Edmund Bonner, had been imprisoned there during the reign of Edward VI for refusing to take the Oath of Supremacy, and on the accession of Elizabeth in 1559 he refused again, and was deprived of his see and committed to the Marshalsea once more. He died in the prison in 1569.

The Marshalsea – second only to the Tower of London among London's prisons at one time – took its name from the fact that its prisoners were committed to it by the Marshalsea Court, presided over by the Marshal of the Royal Household, which dealt with cases of trespass and debt within the royal court. The court's jurisdiction was confined by 1725 to an area within a radius of twelve miles from the royal court, and its activities were much reduced, but it issued writs at the rate of ten thousand a year, and more than a thousand persons a year were said to be committed to what was described in 1777 as 'that old ruinous prison'. One eighteenth-century author entitled his work *Hell in Epitome: or a description of the Marshalsea*. The prison stood in Southwark, close to the present site of Guy's Hospital on the east side of Borough High Street, near the junction with Newcomen Street. The King's Bench Prison was close by, a little farther south, near Mermaid Court. John Stow reported that in the six years up to 1579 a hundred people died in the King's Bench from a contagion known as 'the sickness of the house'.

One of the Marshalsea's prisoners in the early years of the eighteenth century was the public executioner, John Price. He was a brutal, drunken and illiterate fellow who habitually lived beyond his means until, in 1715, he was arrested and thrown into the Marshalsea for debts of seven shillings and sixpence. A new executioner being appointed in his place, Price had no source of income, so could not pay his creditors. He languished in the Marshalsea until the early months of 1718, when he and a fellow prisoner escaped by breaking through a wall. But hardly had Price gained his freedom before he murdered an old woman, and he was hanged by his own successor.

A list of some of the people committed to these prisons over the centuries reads almost like a 'Who's who' of English public life and literature. The dramatists Ben Jonson and George Chapman were committed to the Marshalsea for libel in 1605, having offended James I by their reflections on Scotland in *Eastward Ho!* They were in some danger of having their ears cropped and their noses slit. The founder of the Society of Friends, George Fox, spent a night in the Marshalsea in 1654, and his disciple William Penn, founder of Pennsylvania, was in the Fleet from 1707 to 1709. John Donne spent a short time in the Fleet in 1602, when it was discovered that he, aged twenty-nine, had contracted a secret marriage with a minor, a girl named Ann More, aged sixteen, who was his patron's niece, without her father's knowledge. Another inmate of the Fleet was William Wycherley, who spent seven years there until James II, delighted with his play *The Plain Dealer*, ordered that his debts should be paid out of the privy purse.

All three of these prisons were used almost exclusively for debtors by this time. William Hogarth's father, Richard, was confined to the Fleet for debt when his coffee-house failed, and the family lived there for five years, William's mother selling patent medicines to scrape a little money together. William was only a boy at the time, and the experience marked him for life. John Cleland wrote *Fanny Hill* whilst incarcerated in the Fleet for debt between 1748 and 1752. The proceeds from the book enabled him to pay his creditors. Thomas Dekker spent some years in the King's Bench for debt, and John

Aubrey tells us that Dr John Pell, the Cambridge mathematician and diplomat, was 'cast into the King's Bench prison for Debt Sept 7, 1680'.

The King's Bench Prison was moved to a new site in 1758, on the east side of St George's Fields, at the junction of Borough Road and Scovell Road, near the southern end of Borough High Street. Tobias Smollett was imprisoned there for libel in the following year, and was visited by his friends Goldsmith and Garrick. He committed various characters in his novels to the debtors' prisons – Roderick Random to the Marshalsea; Peregrine Pickle to the Fleet – and described the King's Bench as 'a neat little regular town, consisting of one street, surrounded by a very high wall, including an open piece of ground, which may be termed a garden, where the prisoners take the air and amuse themselves with a variety of diversions'. Another inmate characterised it more succinctly as 'a mappe of misery'.

Creditors could have people clapped into these prisons without trial, even for trifling amounts, but the prisoners were kept there at their creditors' expense. Most such prisoners were confined for small debts and did not remain long, but others spent long periods in the prisons and fared well or ill according to their status. They were confined either until they could clear their debts or until they were discharged as insolvents by Act of Parliament. The 'better class' of debtors could rent apartments from the prison keepers and live there with their wives and families. Corruption was rife. Moses Pitt told in his *Cry of the Oppressed* in 1691 that he had to pay the Keeper of the Fleet two pounds, four shillings and sixpence to get a room on the 'gentleman's side'. The legal fee was fourpence.

The most famous prisoner of the King's Bench was the Member of Parliament for Aylesbury, John Wilkes, who was sentenced in 1768 to twenty-two months and fines of a thousand pounds for obscene and seditious libels.

Large crowds gathered along the route as he made his way from Westminster Hall to the King's Bench prison. Wilkes was the champion of the ordinary people, and on 10 May a hostile crowd of his supporters gathered round the prison. It was quickly rumoured that they were intent on attacking the building and freeing not only Wilkes but all the other prisoners, too. A troop of horse and a hundred men of the Third Regiment of Foot Guards were promptly dispatched to the prison by the government. A justice of the peace read the Riot Act, and was greeted by a hail of stones from the jeering mob. One man was shot by one of the soldiers, causing the crowd to become more furious still. The soldiers were ordered to open fire, and in what became known as the 'St George's Fields Massacre', several people were killed, including a woman selling oranges. Many more were injured. That night, mobs pulled down the houses of two magistrates and demonstrated outside the House of Lords. Wilkes's fines were paid by his supporters, and he lived in an 'apartment de luxe' in the so-called State House, dining with visiting friends and relations, and receiving gifts of wine, pork, salmon and game, not to mention money. He was also able to receive his mistress, Mrs Bernard, and enjoy the generosity of other young women.

The wardens ran coffee shops and drinking houses inside the prison precincts, and further supplemented their incomes by selling privileges, such as freedom to leave the prisons during the daytime, or even to live outside the prison walls 'within the rules', some prisons having houses within the boundaries of their property but outside the prison walls. In April 1776, the Fleet had three hundred and nineteen prisoners, of whom seventy-eight lived 'within the rules'. The King's Bench, in January of the same year, had four hundred and forty-four prisoners, of whom eighty lived outside the prison walls. In 1763, John Howard computed the total number of debtors in the three London prisons at eight hundred and fifty-three, of whom thirty-four were women. Many were imprisoned for debts of less than ten pounds.

Howard saw tradesmen from outside playing at skittles, fives and other games with prisoners in the courtyard of the Fleet: 'I saw among them several butchers and others from the market; who are admitted here as at another public house'. The debtors could carry on their businesses whilst they were confined, and their homes and property outside were protected. Many debtors thus made a mockery of the law by living as comfortably in prison as they did at home, with no incentive whatever to pay their debts.

The poorer prisoners, however, had a very different experience. They lived in filthy and overcrowded cells or wards riddled with gaol fever. That gaol fever flourished in the Fleet was hardly surprising when, as Macaulay described the vicinity, black torrents 'roared down Snow Hill and Ludgate Hill, bearing to Fleet Ditch a vast tribute of animal and vegetable filth from the stalls of butchers and greengrocers'. These hopeless debtors might be clapped in irons, or thrown into cells with prisoners suffering from smallpox, or into dungeons that lay over sewers filled with corpses. At the King's Bench a dozen or more were crowded at night into cold, foul cells no more than six feet square. In 1714 two or three inmates a day were dying in the Marshalsea, and it was reported by the Parliamentary Committee a few years later that three hundred had died there in a period of less than three months. Some died of starvation.

Prostitution and drunkenness were routine in the debtors' as well as other prisons – the Fleet was said at one time to be the biggest brothel in the metropolis, and there were 'few hours of the night without riots and drunkenness'. The King's Bench prison had thirty gin-shops at one period, and John Howard was told at the

Marshalsea that 'one Sunday in the summer 1775, about six hundred pots of beer were brought in from a public house in the neighbourhood (Ashmore's), the prisoners not then liking the tapster's beer'. The tapster at the Fleet, as well as some of the prisoners, kept dogs. Prisoners who swore, blasphemed or rioted were liable to be put in the stocks.

Howard observed at the Marshalsea that five of its sixty rooms were 'let to a man who was not a prisoner: in one of them he kept a chandler's shop; in two he lived with his family: the other two he let to prisoners'. The Marshalsea had four rooms for women, but they were not, Howard noted, sufficient for the number, and 'the more modest women complained of the bad company, in which they were confined'.

The Fleet was notorious for its clandestine marriages. 'Fleet marriages', sometimes between minors, were conducted there without banns or licences by penurious parsons in the prison's squalid tenements, and children were brought up in them. These marriages were popular because they were cheap, and couples came in off the streets to be married in the Fleet prison. The poet and clergyman Charles Churchill had made a Fleet marriage with a girl named Scott in 1748, when he was seventeen, six years before he took holy orders. Shady clergymen could usually be bribed to back-date registrations of marriage in order to legitimise children born out of wedlock.

The Fleet was also known as a receiving house for smuggled or stolen goods, because smugglers were confined there, as well as debtors. When excise men attempted to conduct searches, they were either prevented by hostile and violent inmates from gaining access, or their efforts were foiled by the prisoners' simple expedient of bribing the keeper and turnkeys to help them hide the contraband.

During the Gordon Riots, in June 1780, the Fleet and

King's Bench prisons were totally destroyed by the mobs, who set fire to them after freeing the prisoners. When a fire engine arrived at the Fleet, the crowd pushed the engine into the flames. Some of the poorer inmates of the King's Bench were less than happy at being ejected. Dickens described them in *Barnaby Rudge*:

> The gates of the King's Bench and Fleet Prisons being opened at the usual hour, were found to have notices affixed to them, announcing that the rioters would come that night to burn them down . . . There were some broken men among these debtors who had been in jail so long, and were so miserable and destitute of friends, so dead to the world, and utterly forgotten and uncared for, that they implored their jailers not to set them free, and to send them, if need be, to some other place of custody. But they, refusing to comply, lest they should incur the anger of the mob, turned them into the streets, where they wandered up and down hardly remembering the ways untrodden by their feet so long, and crying – such abject things those rotten-hearted jails had made them – as they slunk off in their rags, and dragged their slipshod feet along the pavement.

The two ruined prisons were again rebuilt, and the Marshalsea moved to new premises a little to the south in 1799. It was in the New Marshalsea that John Dickens, Charles's father, was confined for a debt of forty pounds in 1824. Charles, aged twelve, was working in a blacking factory and lodging in nearby Lant Street, and he went daily to the Marshalsea for his breakfast and supper, his mother and her other children having moved in with his father. John Dickens and his family lived in the best prison style in the Marshalsea for three months, but the experience made a profound impression on the young Charles, and the debtors' prisons appeared later in his novels – the Fleet most notably in *Pickwick Papers*; the King's Bench in *David Copperfield*; the Marshalsea in *Little Dorrit*.

'Most of our readers will remember', Dickens wrote in *Pickwick Papers*, 'that, until within a very few years past, there was a kind of iron cage in the wall of the Fleet Prison, within which was posted some man of hungry looks, who, from time to time, rattled a money-box, and exclaimed, in a mournful voice, "Pray, remember the poor debtors; pray, remember the poor debtors".' But it was Dickens's own vivid childhood memories of the Marshalsea which provided the best impression of these institutions, in *Little Dorrit*. William Dorrit is confined there, in a 'living grave', for twenty-three years, by an unjust law, and has become the 'Father of the Marshalsea'.

The Fleet and Marshalsea prisons were closed in 1842 on their amalgamation with the King's Bench (renamed Queen's Bench) to which all their prisoners were removed. Their keepers were compensated by the government for their loss of profitable businesses, and the Fleet's old buildings were demolished a few years later. The Queen's Bench prison became a military gaol for a time, when imprisonment for debt was more or less abolished, but it was demolished in 1879. In 1856 Dickens had noted that he had been 'to the Borough yesterday morning before going to Gadshill, to see if I could find any ruins of the Marshalsea. Found a great part of the original building – now "Marshalsea Place".' The Marshalsea had been sold in 1842 for use as business premises, and was finally demolished in 1897.

3
PROVINCIAL FORTRESSES

The horrors of imprisonment in Britain were by no means confined to London. The account by George Fox, the 'Quaker', of his time in the so-called 'Doomsdale Tower' at Launceston, in 1656, rivals almost anything, barring physical torture, written about the Tower of London or Newgate. The stone building utilised as a county gaol stood beside the north gate of the outer bailey of Launceston Castle, and was entered by an arched door from the gateway passage:

> The place was so noisome, that it was said few that went in ever came out again alive. There was no house of office in it; and the excrements of the prisoners that from time to time had been put there, had not been carried out (as we were told) for many years. So that it was all like mire, and in some places to the top of the shoes in water and piss; and [the jailer] would not let us cleanse it, nor suffer us to have beds or straw to lie on. At night some friendly people of the town brought us a candle and a little straw, and we burnt a little of our straw to take away the stink. The thieves lay over our heads, and the head jailer in a room by them, over us also. Now it seems the smoke went up into the jailer's room, which put him into such a rage that he took the pots of excrements of the thieves, and poured them through a hole upon our heads in Doomsdale, whereby we were so bespattered that we could not touch ourselves or one another. And the stink increased upon us, so that what with that, and what with smoke, we had nearly been choked and smothered. We had the stink under our feet before, but now we had it on our heads and backs also; and he, having quenched our straw with the filth he poured down, had

made a great smother in the place . . . In this manner were we fain to stand all night, for we could not sit down, the place was so full of filthy excrements. A great while he kept us after this manner before he would let us cleanse it, or suffer us to have any victuals brought in but what we had through the grate . . . The head-jailer, we were informed, had been a thief, and was branded in the hand and in the shoulder; his wife, too, had been branded in the hand for some wickedness. The under-jailer had been branded in the hand and shoulder; and his wife in the hand also. Colonel Bennet, who was a Baptist teacher, having purchased the jail and lands belonging to the Castle, had placed the head-jailer therein. The prisoners, and some wild people, talked of spirits that haunted Doomsdale, and how many had died in it; thinking perhaps to terrify us therewith. But I told him that if all the spirits and devils in hell were there, I was over them in the power of God, and feared no such thing.

Here we have, in a paragraph, a concise summary of all the evils of English prisons in the seventeenth century, which saw precious little improvement by the end of the eighteenth. The local prisons in those days were simply places where criminals could be put out of the way for a time and forgotten. The gaols were privately owned and run for profit. The prison at Halifax was owned by the Duke of Leeds; that at Chesterfield by the Duke of Portland. The keepers were corrupt landlords who made profits by extorting money from their prisoners. The Earl of Derby made thirteen pounds a year from his gaol at Macclesfield.

Fox's contemporary, John Bunyan, spent twelve years in prison in Bedford (John Howard's home town), but did not, it seems, have such a hard time as Fox. Nevertheless, he knew, or imagined, what hellholes prisons could be, for he wrote famously of Giant Despair throwing his captives, Christian and Hopeful, into a 'very dark dungeon' in Doubting Castle, 'nasty and stinking to the spirits of these two men', where they lay for several days 'without one bit of bread, or drop of drink, or light, or any to ask how they did ...', and where their captor beat them mercilessly and counselled them to do away with themselves 'with knife, halter or poison', seeing that they were 'never like to come out of that place'.

More than a hundred years after Fox's experience, John Howard visited Launceston, and did not find things greatly improved. The prison was, he found,

> a room or passage, 23½ feet by 7½ feet, with only one window 2 feet by 1½: and three dungeons or cages opposite the window ... They were all very offensive ... I once found the prisoners chained two or three together. Their provision was put down to them through a hole (9 inches by 8) in the floor of the room above (used as a chapel); and those who served them there, often caught the fatal fever. At my first visit I found the keeper, his assistant, and all the prisoners but one (an old soldier) sick of it: and heard that a few years before, many prisoners had died of it; and the keeper and his wife in one night.

The stone castles of both the great northern capitals were Norman in origin, Lancaster's rising on the southern bank of the River Lune, and York's on the eastern bank of the Ouse. Both fortresses were utilised as prisons long before some of their buildings were converted for use as county gaols, at York in the eighteenth century and at Lancaster in the nineteenth. Prior to these conversions, the castle prisons were medieval dungeons, and their most famous prisoners had been the Lancashire witches and George Fox, in Lancaster's case, and Dick Turpin, in York's.

In March 1612, four women were arrested as suspected witches and committed to the Well Tower of Lancaster Castle, to await trial. Led by Elizabeth Southerns, known locally as Old Demdyke, and Anne Whittle, known as Chattox, both about eighty years old, these women and other reputed witches seem to have conducted a reign of terror over the gullible inhabitants of the Pendle Forest area of Lancashire. The other members of the coven met to discuss ways of freeing the four in prison, and planned to murder the jailer and blow up the building. But during the following weeks, more of them were arrested, until twenty were in the castle awaiting trial. Elizabeth Southerns died in prison. Of the rest, ten were sentenced to death and hanged in August 1612, among them the widow Chattox, 'a very old withered spent and decreped creature'.

George Fox was confined in Lancaster Castle in 1660, under suspicion of disturbing the peace, being an enemy of the King and a 'chief upholder of the Quakers' sect'. He was released after a time, but was back again a few years later, kept in solitary confinement, the jailer having orders to 'keep me close, and suffer no flesh alive to come at me, for I was not fit . . . to be discoursed with by men'. Fox was put in a room in a tower, so thick with smoke from the rooms below that he was almost smothered, and with the rain coming in on his bed in the winter. 'In this manner did I lie all that long cold winter, till the next Assize; in which time I was so starved with cold and rain, that my body was greatly swelled, and my limbs much numbed'. His friend and patron Margaret Fell, whom he subsequently married, also spent nearly two years in the castle gaol. Fox was eventually transferred to Scarborough Castle, so weak from his experience at Lancaster that he could barely stay on his horse for the journey.

Among those who had suffered in the dungeons at York, meanwhile, was Margaret Clitherow, a Roman Catholic who fell foul of Elizabeth I's persecutions and was pressed to death in York Castle in March 1586, at the age of thirty, for refusing to plead to a charge of harbouring priests. She was one of the many who died for their beliefs during the period of religious persecutions under the Tudors. A widow named Eleanor Hunt had died in York Castle, and a Jesuit priest, Brian Cansfield, died from ill-treatment there in 1645. Many others, priests and laymen, languished in the dungeons of both York and Lancaster before being dragged out of their cells to be hanged, drawn and quartered, like John Lockwood, a seminary priest who was executed at York in 1642 at the age of eighty-one.

York Castle had a grim stone-walled cell for the condemned known as 'Pompey's Parlour'. It had a bench in one corner where bodies were quartered after being taken down from the gallows, and the bench was grooved so that the blood ran off. Into this gruesome temporary abode, in late March 1739, came one John Palmer, condemned to death for horse-stealing. He had already been a resident of York Castle for some time, and was now sentenced to hang on 7 April. 'John Palmer', however, was merely the pseudonym of a criminal notorious throughout England – Richard Turpin.

The man known as Palmer had been arrested for shooting a cockerel in the street at Welton, in October of the previous year, but further enquiry had revealed him as a suspected horse-thief who had absconded from Lincolnshire, and after appearing at Beverley Quarter Sessions he had been committed to York Castle. There, he had been identified as Turpin. The gaoler at York, named Griffith, had then clapped him in irons to make sure he did not escape, and the curious flocked from far and wide to peer at the famous prisoner. It was said that the gaoler made a hundred pounds from selling liquor to Turpin and his visitors.

Turpin was hanged at York's Tyburn, the traditional place of execution outside the city walls beyond Micklegate Bar. The hangman may possibly have been one Matthew Blackbourn, who had himself been under sentence of death in the castle a few years earlier, but had 'had his Pardon, being made Hangman'. Turpin was buried in St George's churchyard, where local body-snatchers attempted to steal his corpse.

Thirty-five years after Turpin's execution, John Howard visited York Castle. Extensive rebuilding was going on by that time. The older parts that remained in use had been rebuilt as a debtors' prison in 1705, but the ghastly medieval dungeons were being replaced by new male and female felons' prisons. Howard saw men and boys confined in the old cells, where they were 'locked up at night in winter from fourteen to sixteen hours, straw on the stone floors, no bedsteads. A sewer in one of the passages often makes these parts of the gaol very offensive, and I cannot say they are clean'.

Among the various fees prisoners were required to pay to the gaoler for the privilege of lying in the filthy hole was the following iniquity: 'And every person committed to the gaol for suspicion of felony, or for misdemeanour, if upon his or her trial he or she shall be found not guilty and be thereupon discharged, shall pay to the gaoler for his discharging fee . . . 6s 8d.'

The ancient dungeons at Lancaster, meanwhile, had to serve for another thirty years before this castle, too, underwent conversion into a shire hall and county gaol. And even now visitors can see some of the macabre instruments and devices that made Lancaster Castle a hellhole for many of those unfortunate prisoners confined to it. There is, for instance, the iron clamp used to hold firm a prisoner's forearm, and the branding-iron with which an 'M' was burned into the palm of his (or her) hand, to signify 'malefactor'. They were last put to use as late as 1811.

The chief exponent of branding at that time was the executioner Edward Barlow, commonly known as 'Old Ned'. Barlow was a Welshman who served Lancaster for around a quarter of a century, when it had become known as the 'hanging town' because of the frequency of the death sentences pronounced there. (This was partly due to the fact that Lancaster served as the assize court for Liverpool and Manchester, as well as the rest of Lancashire.) Barlow was as great a villain as any of those he dispatched. One account says that he was guilty of 'nearly every vile act, was many times convicted, and twice sentenced to transportation for life'. He was loathed by the local populace, and was often physically assaulted and pelted with 'missiles of the foulest description'. In March 1806, Barlow was convicted of stealing a horse, and was sentenced to death, but the sentence was commuted to ten years' imprisonment, and Old Ned died in Lancaster Castle in December 1812.

At one time, those condemned to death in the locality had usually been taken from Lancaster Castle to a gallows known as the 'Tyburn shape' on Lancaster Moor, overlooking Morecambe Bay. Later, the castle itself was the scene of public executions. There was a so-called 'drop room' on an upper floor, with a recess in the outside wall below it, and spectators could view the hangings as the condemned were suspended from a beam on the floor above to struggle against death by strangulation and then dangle for an hour in this corner of the castle walls.

After Barlow's demise, the Sheriff of Lancashire took to engaging executioners from outside the county, rather than employing his own man. William Calcraft, the London executioner, travelled all the way to Lancaster on more than one occasion. Yorkshire, however, which had employed its own native hangman from time immemorial, continued to do so for another sixty-five years. Among the other relics at Lancaster is a ghastly wooden 'hanging chair' on castors, which was made specially in 1828 in order to execute Jane Scott, who had been sentenced to death for the murder of her mother, but was physically incapable of walking from her cell and standing up on the scaffold.

A fellow from Thirsk named John Curry, a.k.a.

Wilkinson, was in prison in York Castle in 1802 when a vacancy arose for a hangman. He was offered a reduction of his life sentence in return for accepting it. He used to fortify himself with gin for his grim task, and was frequently jeered by the crowds at executions. In January 1813 Curry hanged fourteen Luddite rioters for their part in the famous raid on Cartwright's mill at Rawfolds – the incident described in Charlotte Brontë's novel *Shirley*. The trial judge remarked that because of their number, they 'might hang more comfortably on two beams'. Curry hanged seven of them at eleven o'clock in the morning, and the other seven at half-past one.

In 1821 Curry was roughly handled by the mob whilst making his way from the castle to the city gaol, and drank so much to calm his nerves that he was scarcely able to climb on to the scaffold. On another occasion, he fell through the trap himself whilst carrying out a multiple execution, and was badly bruised when he emerged to roars of laughter from the spectators. He retired in 1835, after more than thirty years of hanging Yorkshire's criminals. He was succeeded by a coal-porter named Nathaniel Howard, and then by one Thomas Askern of Maltby, before Yorkshire resigned itself to engaging the men recommended by the Home Office.

After the abolition of public executions, both York and Lancaster castles were eventually superseded as hanging prisons, by Armley Gaol, Leeds, and Strangeways, Manchester, respectively, although the last execution at Lancaster did not take place until 1910, and the execution shed remained *in situ* until 1965, when the death penalty was abolished. William Marwood, the first practitioner of the 'long drop', hanged a man named Vincent Knowles Walker at York Castle in May 1878.

Two treadwheels were installed at Lancaster in the first quarter of the nineteenth century. At about the same time the last major extension of the prison was completed with the building of the Female Penitentiary. Lancaster was one of the prisons which continued to employ the useless and demoralising punishment of 'shot drill' right up until 1878, when it was abolished by the state on taking over the responsibility for running county and borough gaols. Prisoners were made to stand in concentric circles, each man with a twenty-four-pound shot between his feet. At the order to move, each prisoner had to lift the heavy shot waist high, step forward six paces, put the shot down, and return to his starting point, where he found another shot waiting for him, deposited by the man behind him in the next circle. This painfully exhausting process would go on for four hours at a time, and had a tendency to cause ruptures.

Lancaster Castle was the scene of a mystery in 1911 when the keeper of the castle, William Bingham, aged seventy-three, and his daughter Margaret and son James all died within seven months of one another. When James died, traces of arsenic were found in his organs, and suspicion led to the exhumation of his father and half-sister. Arsenic was found to be present in both corpses. It was agreed that all three had been murdered, and suspicion fell on William Bingham's surviving daughter Edith, who had lived in the castle all her life, her father having become keeper before she was born. Edith was mentally subnormal, illiterate and troublesome, but after a trial lasting three days, she was acquitted on all charges, and the mystery of the Bingham family remains unsolved. Edith Bingham spent her last years in Lancaster Moor asylum, dying there in 1944.

York's castle prison has long since gone, metamorphosed into the Castle Museum. One of its cells for debtors held George Hudson, the 'Railway King', one of the last persons imprisoned for debt in England. Despite being an infirm old man of sixty-five, he was arrested at Whitby in July 1865 and brought to York on one of his own trains, to be locked up in the damp cells of the castle gaol for more than three months.

Lancaster Castle, the property of the Crown, was closed as a prison during the First World War, being surplus to requirements then, but it was sublet to the Home Office again in 1954, and remains in use, notwithstanding the long catalogue of horrors perpetrated there which was related to the House of Commons in 1812 by Sir Francis Burdett. Lancaster has Britain's highest prison walls, rising to more than fifty feet in places. There are hopes that the prison will be closed down finally in the near future, but such hopes seem unduly optimistic in the light of the government's apparent determination to lock up *more* offenders, not fewer, as most modern reformers advocate.

4

COLDBATH FIELDS HOUSE
OF CORRECTION, LONDON

As he went through Cold-Bath Fields, he saw
A solitary cell;
And the Devil was pleased, for it gave him a hint
For improving his prisons in Hell.

Coleridge's much-quoted quatrain from 'The Devil's
Thoughts', published in 1799, referred to the penitentiary at Clerkenwell which was commonly known in the
London underworld, throughout its existence, as 'the
Bastille', or 'the Steel' for short. It was designed by Jacob
Leroux and Charles Middleton on the general principles
proposed by John Howard, and built between 1788 and
1794 on a site close to the Fleet River, near the present
junction of Farringdon Road and Roseberry Avenue,
where the Mount Pleasant postal sorting office stands.

The prison, which originally had two hundred and
thirty-two cells, was a realisation of the 1779 Penitentiary Act, intended to provide for rehabilitation through a
combination of solitary confinement and hard labour,
when the American War of Independence had limited
the scope for transportation, and the frightening extent
of gaol fever had made the provision of ostensibly
healthier buildings essential. With subsequent extension, Coldbath Fields became the largest prison in
Britain, with accommodation for nearly fifteen hundred.
It stood in a district of rapidly rising population in the
wake of the Industrial Revolution. It was also, conse-
quently, at the centre of an area with a growing crime
rate, though two of its early inmates were no ordinary
back-street criminals. At the one extreme, the Irish

Colonel Edward Despard was committed to it after the discovery of his conspiracy to assassinate George III. At the other, a man named Patterson fell victim to Pitt's pettiness after Mr Patterson had, according to Sheridan, painted a trading sign 'Pitt and Patterson' on his shop cart, as a protest against the income tax bill. Asked to explain himself, the satirical rogue said that although Mr Pitt had no interest in the business, he had a share of the profits.

Almost from the beginning, Coldbath Fields was a source of scandal and corruption. It was harsh, squalid and – despite the intentions – unhealthy. Some prisoners were allegedly fed on cat meat. Built as the House of Correction for the County of Middlesex, but with a contribution to its cost from the City of London, which shared its facilities, it was soon a mockery of almost everything that John Howard had thought desirable in penal reform. The Middlesex magistrates appointed as its governor one Thomas Aris, whose qualification for the job was that he had been a baker at Clerkenwell, and who treated the post as an opportunity to feather his own nest, charging fees for beds and saving costs by reducing the prisoners' diet to bread and water. An establishment that was meant to enforce discipline and instil terror, by means of solitary confinement, soon became overcrowded, with two prisoners sleeping in one bed in some of the small cells, and in the winter, the place was cold and damp. The convicts had to contend with 'swarms of mice'. Aris had prisoners committed to the dark punishment cells of the prison for weeks at a time for trivial misdemeanours, and allowed one – a vagrant – to die in a cold cell for lack of adequate food, clothing and medical attention. There was a riot in the prison chapel in 1798, when some prisoners escaped. The rest were promptly chained up.

In May 1800, a fourteen-year-old girl named Mary Rich claimed to have been raped. Her assailant was allowed bail whilst his victim was confined in Coldbath Fields for more than a month. By the time the case came to court, the girl was starving, and fainted during her testimony. She had been kept on bread and water in solitary confinement. When Sir Francis Burdett brought her case to public notice, the chairman of the Middlesex justices, William Mainwairing, MP, said that Mary Rich was a common whore and had been fed better in prison than at home – a curious reason, as Sheridan pointed out in the Commons, for defending inhumanity in the gaol. Yet defenders of the Coldbath Fields system included people such as William Wilberforce and the religious writer and philanthropist Hannah More.

In August of the same year, a further riot occurred. Convicts had been observed gathering together in the exercise yard and muttering darkly among themselves, and had to be forced into their cells at gunpoint. Many of the cells were outward-facing, and the prisoners attracted the attention of the local community by staging a rumpus, shouting 'Murder!' and 'We're being starved!' from the windows, and banging on their doors and bedsteads. Soon there was a crowd of some five thousand outside the prison walls, and both prisoners and spectators were shouting 'Pull down the Bastille!' Aris called for help from Bow Street Runners and local volunteers, and after several hours, the disturbances were brought to an end. Twenty ringleaders were taken to the punishment cells in chains.

There was another, similar riot two years later, when the women prisoners were especially turbulent, some of them being gagged and hauled in chains to the punishment cells. Coldbath Fields was the prison where London's prostitutes regularly found themselves.

Alexander Stephens, foreman of the Middlesex grand jury, inspected Coldbath Fields in 1807 and found there a French officer, Chevalier du Blin, who had been arrested for spying nearly three years before and held

46

ever since in solitary confinement. He had gone out of his mind, shouting and tearing his clothing, and insisting that he could hear his wife and children being tortured in a nearby cell. He was transferred to St Luke's Hospital for the Insane.

A few years later, John Hunt, co-editor of the radical Sunday newspaper *The Examiner*, was sent to Coldbath Fields when he and his brother, Leigh Hunt, were sentenced by Lord Chief Justice Ellenborough to two years' imprisonment for publishing a libel on the Prince Regent (they had described him as 'a fat Adonis of fifty').

Stephens also found debtors incarcerated with the worst felons, some prisoners held in solitary confinement whilst awaiting trial, and others receiving short rations. There was evidence that Aris's son had been sexually assaulting female prisoners. When Sheridan brought these details to the attention of the House of Commons, a commission of enquiry was appointed, and found the various allegations to be true, but nothing was done. Despite all the outrages, Aris remained as governor, though he was eventually dismissed, some years afterwards. He died in poverty.

Coldbath Fields was at length converted to the 'silent system', in which prisoners were allowed to mix together during daylight working hours, but were strictly forbidden to speak or communicate in any way. The author of this new regime was George Laval Chesterton, a retired army officer and Peninsular War veteran, who was appointed in 1829 and introduced the rule of silence in 1834, when he had had time to make his wardens into a disciplined force of men instead of the corrupt turnkeys he had found on his arrival. Among their perks had been the taking of bribes to admit male convicts into the women's quarters via a hidden trapdoor.

Chesterton described his method, which was soon copied by many other prisons:

> Prisoners are kept under constant and secret inspection day and night, lights being burned in the sleeping rooms all night and night watches on the alert; every movement of the prisoners is made so as to prevent their faces being turned to each other; they are never allowed to congregate or cluster together; they move in solitary lines in single file.

Enforcing this rule required a large staff of wardens. By the 1860s, the prison had a ratio of one warder to every thirteen prisoners, compared with one to every seventeen at Pentonville. Prison rules and Biblical injunctions were posted round the buildings, such as a warning against swearing, which seemed superfluous, considering that prisoners were punished for speaking at all. No prisoner in Chesterton's gaol was referred to by name. Prison numbers were used, in the belief that convicts could be reformed by a kind of enforced alienation from their past lives and personalities. They were locked in their cells for twelve hours a day, and were allowed only one letter and one visit every three months. Their meals consisted of bread, meat and potatoes for dinner on four days of the week, and bread and soup on the other three. They were given bread and cocoa for breakfast, and bread and gruel for supper.

The regime was impartial in its unrelenting harshness. One man hanged himself in his cell after being committed to Coldbath Fields for seven days because he was unable to pay a trifling fine for a trivial offence. A local undertaker had a profitable contract with the prison to bury those who died there in a cemetery at Bethnal Green.

The convicts were generally employed on picking oakum, the punishing and soul-destroying daily routine of unravelling old ropes, to be used for caulking the decks of ships. Men under sentences of hard labour would be given up to six pounds of old rope, or 'junk', to pick. The rope, sometimes tarred, cut and blistered their fingers, so that until their skin became hardened and accustomed to it, the job was very painful. The convicts did this work sitting closely together in rows in a large workshop, under the supervision of watchful warders. Prisoners caught talking might be flogged, or sent to the dark punishment cells, where they were clapped in irons and kept on bread and water.

Unproductive hard labour was almost an article of faith with Chesterton, who deplored what he called the 'mawkish theories' of reformers who wanted to remove 'salutary terrors' from the prisons. He saw hard labour as a punishment, not as training for useful work. One of the activities the prisoners were subjected to was known as 'shot drill'. For hours on end convicts were made to pick up cannon balls from one point in an exercise yard, carry them to another and put them down, and then repeat the useless process, just as at Lancaster.

By this time, the prison had also been equipped with a treadwheel. This form of punishment had first been introduced at Gloucester in 1811. The civil engineer William Cubitt invented a new type of treadmill a few years later, and within four years his machines had been installed in more than fifty prisons around the country. The idea was generally to utilise prison labour as a useful source of energy. The treadmill, a huge cylinder with slatted steps along its length, ranging in size to accommodate six to eighteen prisoners working side-by-side in separate stalls, could be used to raise water or grind corn, or to supply power to other machinery. But in some cases, the infernal machine known as the 'everlasting staircase' was simply a form of torture with no end-product. In the case of Coldbath Fields, prisoners merely drove a useless fan which regulated the effort necessary to turn it. The labour of 'grinding the wind', as the convicts called it, was extremely exhausting, because – as a warder explained – 'the men can get no firm tread, like, from the steps always sinking away from under their feet . . .' Male prisoners were made to do this useless work for more than four hours a day, with fifteen-minute rests at intervals, and they had to perform the equivalent of climbing more than a vertical mile and a quarter.

The treadwheel – which the government of the day considered an 'excellent instrument of corrective discipline' – substituted a new terror for the abandoned horrors of solitary confinement, and became the most feared aspect of prison life almost throughout the nineteenth century. Already being described by mid-century as a 'relic of ignorance and barbarity', the treadwheel was injurious to the health of women, and to many of the men. Sweat poured from them as they laboured in the heat generated in the semi-enclosed stalls or compartments. The machine caused ruptures and varicose swellings, rheumatism and respiratory illnesses. One prisoner at Coldbath Fields fell into the machinery and was mangled to death. Elizabeth Fry observed that there was 'more cruelty in our Gaols than I have ever seen before'. Henry Mayhew described a treadwheel as having the appearance of 'the stalls in a public urinal', and its male operators had another sensitive reason for hating it – not for nothing did they call it the 'cockchafer'. Some convicts would go to almost any lengths to evade the treadwheel, such as swallowing soap or large quantities of salt to induce fever.

By 1848, women prisoners were being employed in the workshops instead of on the treadwheels, of which Coldbath Fields now had several, but an article in *Household Words*, probably by Dickens himself, attacked the softening of discipline then being advocated by some reformers, and said that 'it is a satisfaction to me to see the determined thief, swindler, or vagrant, sweating profusely at the treadmill or the crank, and extremely galled to know that he is doing nothing all the time but undergoing *punishment*'. (Nevertheless, the daily work requirement on the treadwheel was reduced;

but it was not until 1898 that the treadmill and the crank were abolished altogether by the Prisons Act.)

In 1850, Coldbath Fields became a prison exclusively for convicted adult males, removing the undesirable fraternisation between male and female criminals, and the obvious evils of imprisoning young boys with hardened and brutal men.

One of the last (temporary) inmates of Coldbath Fields was W. T. Stead, the campaigning editor of the *Pall Mall Gazette*, who spent a short time there in 1885 for abduction, after his ill-judged efforts to bully the government into raising the age of consent for young girls, by setting up a thirteen-year-old, Eliza Armstrong, to be 'bought' as a prostitute, and thus exposing the trade in virgins. Stead was soon transferred to Holloway, then a mixed prison.

In 1887, the Coldbath Fields House of Correction was closed down, as a result of nationalisation, when prisons were removed from local authority responsibility and administration and taken under state control. Pentonville – the Model Prison, as it was originally called – had taken its place.

The American War of Independence presented British prisons with a problem. Transportation to the American colonies, which had been going on since early in the seventeenth century, was suddenly blocked by the rebellious colonists, who refused to have their embryo republic polluted by the English criminal classes. In 1775, transportation came to an abrupt halt, and led to the overcrowding of prisons.

As far as the British authorities were concerned, this was merely a temporary difficulty, and transportation would be resumed as soon as the rebels were crushed. But in the meantime, British gaols could no longer hold all the criminals sentenced to terms of imprisonment at home as alternatives to exile abroad. An answer was found in the rotting old ships at anchor in the Thames and in southern English ports such as Chatham, Portsmouth and Plymouth. Some of these vessels were captured French and Spanish warships. Convicts could be accommodated in the floating hulks and set to hard labour on public works. Within ten years, two thousand men were living in damp and foul men-o'-war and transport vessels at Deptford, Woolwich and elsewhere.

The Act of 1776 authorising the use of redundant ships as prisons delcared that any person whose crime would normally render him liable to transportation should be punished by 'being kept on Board Ships or Vessels properly accommodated for the Security, Employment and Health of the Persons to be confined therein, and by being employed in Hard Labour in the raising Sand, Soil and Gravel from, and cleansing the

River Thames . . .' In practice, however, the health of the prisoners came very low on the list of priorities.

The man appointed by the government to take charge of the prison hulks and their inmates was Duncan Campbell, a private contractor who had twenty years of experience as a transporter of convicts. He was paid £38 per prisoner per year, and he moored his first two ships, *Justitia* and *Censor*, near Woolwich, where he received his first convicts in August 1776.

Other vessels were quickly added to the small fleet of prison ships. The *Leviathan* – a ninety-gun warship – had been one of Nelson's fleet at Trafalgar. Another of Nelson's ships, *Bellerophon*, was moored at Sheerness. This seventy-four-gun man-o'-war had brought Napoleon to England, after Waterloo, en route for St Helena. One of Captain Cook's ships, the *Discovery*, was also used as a prison hulk for ten years before she was broken up at Woolwich. But the once-proud ships of oak soon became floating slums, sinking into mud banks at low tide, alive with vermin, and stinking with the foul air resulting from overcrowding and lack of ventilation.

The hulks on the Thames lay anchored in close single file, the bows of one almost nudging the stern of the next, and convicts were brought to them shackled together. After their hair had been cropped, they were given baths in cold water and dressed in prison uniform. Once on the hulks, prisoners had irons weighing fourteen pounds riveted to their right ankles, as a deterrent to escape by swimming ashore. The parliamentarian H. G. Bennett saw a thirteen-year-old boy aboard the *Leviathan* at Portsmouth in 1817, crawling about in double fetters, though most adult convicts wore only single ones.

The prisoners slept in hammocks slung close together in crowded decks. The orlop or lowest desk of the *Brunswick* at Chatham accommodated 460 prisoners at night in a space less than five feet in height and 125 feet in length by 40 feet at the broadest part of the deck.

Diseases brought aboard the cramped, airless and infected ships spread rapidly. John Howard noted the 'sickly looks' of convicts on the *Justitia* in October 1776. 'Many had no shirts, some no waistcoats . . . some no stockings and some no shoes . . .' When he asked one man, who looked very ill, how he was, the reply came that he was ready to sink into the earth. Of 632 convicts taken on board the *Justitia* in the first eighteen months, 176 died. Typhus and cholera were among the commonest scourges, with scurvy, scrofula, dysentery and diarrhoea also prevalent.

When a convict died, his corpse might well be sold for a few pounds to one or other of the anatomists' agents who habitually hung about the docks. This trade saved the cost and trouble of a funeral and, besides, the fear of infection from the hulks was so great that one naval chaplain had been known to conduct a burial service from a distance of a mile, waving his handkerchief from the deck of his ship to signal the moment to lower the coffin into the grave.

Sir Jerome Fitzpatrick, an agitator for better conditions for convicts sentenced to transportation, referred to some prisoners on the hulks as 'infirm and diseased, completely Blind, crippled and so advanced in Age that no sort of profit can be made from their labour . . .' Yet a Committee of Enquiry appointed by the government to report on conditions aboard the prison ships came up with the conclusion that they were 'convenient, airy, and healthy'. The witnesses whose evidence the committee relied upon were – apart from John Howard – Campbell and his officers and cronies.

The hulks on the Thames were popularly known as 'Campbell's Academy', where young prisoners were educated in criminal ways by the more experienced convicts. Patrick Colquhoun, a London magistrate, wrote that he had seldom known of an instance of a released convict returning to honest industry.

> ... on the contrary, many of them have been detected immediately afterward in the commission of new crimes, from which it may be inferred that this species of punishment has not answered the intentions of the legislature so far as relates to the reformation of the convicts; but the chief cause of the general corruption of morals, which is so apparent, has been traced to the indiscriminate mixture of hardened and irreclaimable thieves with country convicts who, under other circumstances, might have been reclaimed, but with so many evil examples before them too often become as hardened at the period of their discharge as the worst class of felons, thereby rendering the establishment a complete seminary of vice and wickedness.

Howard noted in June 1788 that there were three hundred and sixty-six convicts aboard a prison ship, the *Dunkirk*, at Plymouth dock. 'Three miserable objects, for attempting to break out, were let down into a dreadful, dark and deep hole at the bottom of the ship, where they lay, almost naked, upon a little straw; but, having been there confined for some weeks, upon their earnest entreaties, I obtained their release.' A Scottish convict, Thomas Watling, wrote afterwards that he had seen 'so much wanton cruelty practised on board the *English* hulks, on poor wretches, without the least colour of justice, what may I not infer? – *French* Bastille, nor *Spanish* Inquisition, could not centre more of horrors.'

Those who were fit for work were employed in chain-gangs, raising sand for ships' ballast, or ashore under armed guard, working at stone-breaking in the quarries. They were fed on rations of oatmeal and cheese, meat and small beer, and sometimes on bread and water, but did not always get their full entitlement of even this inadequate fare, since cooks and ship's crew would help themselves to food intended for the convicts – particularly the meat delivered on board. Howard saw mouldly biscuit, green in colour, being distributed to the convicts from sacks.

Fighting and drunkenness were only the least of the horrors that occurred below decks at night, when the hatches had been secured. Jeremy Bentham remarked that it was a matter of course for convicts taken aboard the hulks at Woolwich to be raped. A convict on the *Portland*, at Portsmouth, wrote that the 'horrible crime of sodomy rages so shamefully throughout that the Surgeon and myself have been more than once threatened with assassination for straining to put a stop to it . . .' Venereal disease was almost universal.

Breaches of discipline were usually punished by flogging. A convict named Woolley, on board the first-rater *Ganymede*, was flogged several times for being in possession of tobacco, and once bit the top joint off a quartermaster's finger, when the officer put his fingers into Woolley's mouth searching for a concealed quid. The prisoner protested that he could not help his addiction, but the captain said he would cut the flesh off Woolley's back, and the boatswain obeyed his captain's orders.

John Mitchel, an Irish prisoner on the hulks at Bermuda in 1848, described the flogging of three prisoners who had attempted to escape:

> The Governor came this morning in person . . . although it was Sunday, to give special orders about the mangling of these culprits tomorrow. It is to be a most solemn and terrific butchery . . .
>
> The laceration is finished. The gangs are sent out to their work after being mustered to witness the example: the troops who were drawn up on the pier have marched home to their barracks: quartermasters and guards have washed the blood-gouts from their arms and faces and arranged their dress again: the three torn carcasses have been carried

down half-dead to the several hospital rooms. Though shut up in my cell all the time, I heard the horrid screams of one man plainly. After being lashed in the *Medway*, they had all been carried to this ship with blankets thrown over their bloody backs: the first of them, after receiving a dozen blows with miserable shrieks, grew weak and swooned: the scourging stopped for about ten minutes while the surgeon used means to revive him – and then he had the remainder of his allowance. He was then carried groaning out of this ship into the *Coromandel*, instantly stripped again, and cross-scarified with another twenty lashes. The two other men took their punishment throughout in silence – I heard one of them shout once fiercely to the quartermaster, 'Don't cut below the mark, damn you!' I have been walking up and down my cell gnawing my tongue.

By the end of the century the prisoners held in hulks in the English ports were increasing at the rate of a thousand a year, and among them were boys younger than ten years old. In 1798 two ships at Portsmouth had more than fifty boys of twelve or under among their prisoners. A witness before a House of Lords committee in 1835 mentioned a boy of six on the *Euryalus* at Chatham. He had been convicted of stealing and sentenced to transportation, but died soon after arriving on board. Campbell's services had been dispensed with by this time, and a government inspector was appointed to oversee the management of the hulks, but there were no dramatic changes in conditions as a result.

Lunatics were kept on the hulks unless they proved dangerous, and like the boys, were severely punished for misdemeanours, sometimes with a flogging. There were cases of suicide, and boys would often break their own arms in order to earn a short respite from the appalling conditions by being sent to hospital. The youngsters were known to lay their arms across the edges of bunks or benches and let heavy objects fall on them to cause fractures.

Efforts were made to segregate boys from adults by accommodating them on ships designated for juveniles, so that they should be kept, as one chaplain expressed it, 'from all intercourse with adult prisoners'. Chaplains taught the illiterate to read, but deluded themselves that the 'unfortunate youths who are imprisoned in this ship are enjoying the blessing of a moral and religious education'. The men who eventually emerged from the hulks were usually wrecks themselves.

A convict named Vaux, confined on board the aptly named *Retribution* at Woolwich, later wrote of his experience:

> There were confined in this floating dungeon nearly 600 men, most of them double-ironed; and the reader may conceive the horrible effects arising from the continual rattling of chains, the filth and vermin naturally produced by such a crowd of miserable inhabitants, the oaths and execrations constantly heard among them; and above all the shocking necessity of associating and communicating more or less with so depraved a set of beings . . .

> If I were to attempt a full description of the miseries endured in these ships, I could fill a volume; but I shall sum up by stating that besides robbery from each other, which is as common as cursing and swearing, I witnessed among the prisoners themselves, during the twelve-month I remained with them, one deliberate murder, for which the perpetrator was executed at Maidstone, and one suicide; and that unnatural crimes are openly committed.

A French prisoner – an officer named Dupin – reported to the French government that prisoners of war – Danes, Swedes, Frenchmen and Americans alike – were 'buried alive' in 'floating tombs' on the Medway. Two orderlies on board a hospital ship, *Pegasus*, at Portsmouth, coveted a ring on the swollen finger of a dying French prisoner. Impatience at the length of time it was taking him to expire led them to move him to the mortuary, where he would pass for dead and they could cut off his finger to remove the ring, while he was still alive.

The hulks soon became a national scandal. Riots were frequent, and guards dare not go below to restore order except in armed parties. In one riot in 1786, eight convicts were killed and more than thirty wounded. Overcrowding became so desperate that transportation to Botany Bay began in the following year, to ease the burden on the English prisons. The six famous Tolpuddle Martyrs spent several weeks on board the *York* at Portsmouth in 1834 before being transported to Australia.

By the middle of the nineteenth century, transportation had succeeded in relieving the gaols, and by the time the *Defence* caught fire on the Thames in 1857, and had to be scuttled, no hulks remained in use except a hospital ship, *Unité*, a thirty-six-gun frigate which had been captured from the French. An enquiry carried out by an inspector of prisons, Captain Williams, had at last exposed the true state of affairs on board the hulks, and they were finally abolished in 1857. The last convicts were taken ashore from the *Unité* in 1859. But as I write, nearly a century and a half later, a Prison Department official has said on television that the use of prison ships could be considered again, as a last resort, to help solve the problem of overcrowded gaols.

6

DARTMOOR PRISON

Her Majesty's Prison at Princetown, Devon, commonly known as Dartmoor Prison, was originally built in 1806–9 as barracks to house French prisoners of war. It was the idea of Thomas Tyrwhitt, Member of Parliament, Lord Warden of the Stannaries, and a friend and former secretary of the Prince of Wales. An Essex man, Tyrwhitt had built himself a house on Dartmoor, where he intended to cultivate large areas of land granted to him by the Duchy of Cornwall. He built cottages for his workers, and called his new estate Prince's Town. But he had not reckoned on the harsh inhospitality of the bleak site, nearly 1,500 feet above sea level and exposed on all sides – the wettest place in the southern half of England; to say nothing of its barren resistance to tillage.

Noting the government's concern about the overcrowding of prisons and the rotting hulks at Portsmouth, Tyrwhitt hit on an alternative plan. He proposed to the government that barracks should be built at Prince's Town for the prisoners. Tyrwhitt's own local quarries would supply granite for the purpose, and the prisoners could be employed in building roads and opening up Dartmoor. The proposal was accepted, and Tyrwhitt laid the foundation stone in March 1806.

The architect, David Alexander, designed a range of buildings radiating from the centre like the spokes of a wheel, with five two-storey barrack blocks. It was one of the earliest examples of this type of layout, and was designed to accommodate eight thousand men. The building of the prison, however, was a business nightmare. It cost £127,000, and more than one contractor went bankrupt because of the remoteness of the site and the difficulties of working in the winter climate. Nevertheless, Tyrwhitt was knighted for his enterprise, and the first prisoners arrived in 1809.

The prison soon became overcrowded with nearly nine thousand Frenchmen. Between 1809 and January 1816 there were 1,478 deaths at the prison, some from suicide and some from fighting duels, but most from epidemics. It was said in 1811 that '. . . the air of Dartmoor prison is considered most detrimental to health, noisome and maligant, the soil swampy, ever shrounded in vapour, dreary, wet and aguish, and, indeed, what other can be expected from a spot said to be placed in the midst of 40,000 acres of marshy ground . . .' But whilst one or more prisoners were carving the Latin inscription from Virgil that can still be seen over the entrance arch – PARCERE SVBJECTIS (Pity the Humbled) – others were busy quietly making more useful items, such as English banknotes! Prince's Town enjoyed for a time an artificial prosperity.

Dartmoor during this period – grim as it was – made an appearance in Arthur Conan Doyle's comic novel about a young French officer, *The Exploits of Brigadier Gerard*. 'It was one of the very strangest places in the whole word, for there, in the middle of that great desolate waste, were herded together seven or eight thousand men . . .' The hero of the novel, Colonel Etienne Gerard, escapes from the prison and, aware that if he fails to get away he will be 'thrown into those damp underground cells which are reserved for prisoners who are caught in escaping', sets off with his face to the wind and runs for hours across the moor, in the rain, stumbling and tripping over bushes and brambles until, torn, breathless and bleeding, he reckons he has covered twenty miles, and falls asleep in the heather from exhaustion. When he wakes up, he finds himself outside the prison walls. The wind having changed direction during the night, he has unwittingly run ten miles away and ten miles back. Something of the sort was to become a familiar scenario for would-be escapees from Dartmoor. A quarter of a century later, Conan Doyle's contemporary John Galsworthy made more serious use of the prison in his work.

When the real French prisoners were eventually released from Dartmoor, the prison remained occupied by hundreds of American sailors captured during the war of 1812–14. Many of them died in captivity. The prison was then closed, and stood empty for a long period. There was a proposal, which came to nothing, to turn it into a school of industry, where poor boys from London would be taught a useful trade. Tyrwhitt meanwhile continued to develop Prince Town, as it was now called, building a railway to it from Plymouth. He died in 1833, having sunk thousands of pounds into his grandiose schemes to turn the area into fertile land supporting a thriving community. In 1846, the British Patent Naphtha Company leased some of the buildings for use in converting peat into naphtha, and making candles and mothballs, among other things, but this enterprise was short-lived.

In 1850 the place – more or less derelict for over thirty years – was converted at considerable expense into a civil prison for long-term prisoners, and despite occasional promises to close it down, it remains so to this day. The work of conversion included expanding the accommodation to cope with 1,300 convicts, the first of whom arrived in November of that year.

Within a month, the first escapes had been made from the new prison. Three men got away in December 1850, and although two of them were recaptured within four days, the third, Charles Webster, never came back. The first prison guards were military – eighty men with three officers under the governor, Captain Gambier. Four years later, the military guards were replaced by pensioners, and in 1857, these too were replaced, by civilian guards composed mainly of ex-servicemen. All these experimental regimes eventually gave way to professional warders.

The modernised prison subsequently had four-tier cell-blocks, a hospital block, Catholic and Protestant chapels, workshops and recreation rooms, as well as the necessary offices, stores and maintenance buildings. There were large exercise yards, and the whole was enclosed by a perimeter wall twenty feet high and nearly a mile in circumference.

The convicts, who had to serve the first nine months of their sentences in solitary confinement, were locked in narrow cells of galvanised iron, the only light coming through spaces under the doors by means of which they were fed. They slept on boards, and were each allowed one candle a week for light at night. They were kept short of food, and were liable to find beetles in their bread, tea and suet pudding. Some convicts would greedily consume grass, or their candles, to satisfy their hunger, or even the greasy dubbin with which they were meant to preserve their boots. One convict was said to collect handfuls of earthworms and eat them, sprinkled with salt, when he was out with a working party. Their hair was cropped off to add to the degradation of the prison uniforms. Many of them were 'lifers'. One of the more famous prisoners in the early years was Arthur Orton, the Tichborne claimant, who was sentenced to fourteen years' penal servitude, and became celebrated as 'Sir Roger' among his fellow-convicts.

The only heat in the cell-blocks was provided by a single coke-burning stove in each of them, and in winter, convicts suffered from the bitter cold in this mist-bound and desolate place. Many ex-prisoners of Dartmoor were said to suffer from rheumatism for the rest of their lives. Whilst there, prisoners, serving long sentences of penal servitude, tended to receive few visitors, because of the distance of Princetown from their homes.

No executions were carried out at Dartmoor. In fact, criminals were often sent there after death sentences had been commuted to life imprisonment. But there was corporal punishment, and convicts could be flogged or birched for offences against prison discipline. They were flogged for fighting and disobedience, for swearing and for indecency. There were cases of prisoners being beaten up by warders. A one-armed Irishman, Michael Davitt, a former prisoner who became a Member of Parliament, testified to a Commission of Enquiry that it frequently happened at Dartmoor that 'prisoners were felled by warders, and in punishment cells where I was detained for several months in 1875 and 1876, prisoners have been frequently beaten underneath me in punishment cells in the night time by visiting warders'. The old lags of Dartmoor had a superstition that the jackdaws which frequented the place were the souls of dead warders.

Homosexuality had been rife from the earliest days when prisoners of war occupied the prison. An entry in the records for 10 April 1813 records the punishment of 'M. Giraudi and A. Moine, for attempting to strike Mr. Anquelet, and for being guilty of infamous vices'. Homosexual practices, not only between prisoners, but between prisoners and warders, were later described as the 'curse of the Moor', and the prison chapel was said to be the 'chief breeding-ground of the prison's most pernicious vice'.

The convicts, in their uniforms of khaki trousers, striped jackets and light blue caps, were put to work in gangs which marched out of the prison, under armed guard in earlier times, to reclaim bog land, quarry granite, or break up the quarried stone for making roads. As long as a prisoner was capable of walking, he was considered fit to 'move granite boulders, or carry barrow-loads of turf', even if he was suffering from a rupture or heart disease. In severe weather convicts would work in the prison workshops sewing mailbags. Strict silence was enforced.

At the turn of the century, Dartmoor had more than 1,700 inmates, and its death rate was higher than that of any other prison in the country. There were frequent attempts to escape, some of which were successful. The administration of the prison was inefficient, and discipline lax. But escaping from Dartmoor was a high-risk activity. Men got lost on the moor, or were frozen to death. One fell into a reservoir at night and was drowned. Others fell down disused mineshafts, or into the consuming bogs, whilst being hunted down by police with bloodhounds. Most escapees were captured on the moor or in the towns and villages round its fringes – Tavistock, Ashburton, Moretonhampstead, etc.

Among the many murderers who have spent time at Dartmoor was Steinie Morrison, a Russian-Jewish immigrant who was sentenced to death in 1911 for the murder in London of fellow-immigrant Leon Beron. He was sent to Dartmoor when his sentence was commuted to penal servitude for life by the Home Secretary, Winston Churchill. On his way to Dartmoor, Morrison caused a scene at Waterloo Station, and he is said to have petitioned repeatedly for the death sentence to be carried out on him, in spite of continually protesting his innocence, because he found conditions at Dartmoor so intolerable. He also staged hunger strikes, and was eventually transferred to Parkhurst, on the Isle of Wight, where there were better facilities for dealing with prisoners who were mentally unstable or required medical treatment. He died in January 1921, aged about forty.

Even after more civilised standards were introduced into the prison, such as electricity and central heating (which facilitated conversation between prisoners in their cells by tapping on the pipes in code), Dartmoor remained the most unpopular penal institution in Britain. It was regarded by prisoners, with some justification, as the 'home of forgotten men'. In November 1927, the Home Secretary, Sir William Joynson-Hicks, described the prison, somewhat ambiguously, as a 'cesspool of humanity'. By 1930, the old iron cells had been removed, and the policy of making prisoners spend their first nine months in solitary had been abolished. But in January 1932, the biggest prison mutiny in Britain up to that time occurred at Dartmoor.

It began, as so many prison riots have done, over food. The basis of the prison diet was starch, which maintains weight without producing energy. Prisoners were fed with bread, potatoes and porridge. The latter, known in prison jargon as 'skilly', was made in filthy kitchens during the night and simmered till breakfast time, when it was diluted by rainwater during its journey from the kitchens to the cell-blocks. Other food, left uncovered in the kitchens overnight, was sometimes found to contain mouse-droppings or jackdaw excrement.

The rumblings of discontent exploded into mutiny after a rumour got about that a prisoner had been assaulted by staff. Another prisoner attacked a warder, slashing his face with a razor blade fitted into a piece of wood. Prisoners armed with sticks, shovels and crowbars went on a rampage of destruction, smashing furniture, setting fire to offices, immobilising the prison fire engine, and raiding stores for beer, spirits and cigarettes. Some men attempted to escape, but none succeeded, and the riot was quelled the same day, after twelve hours. Prison officers had entered the mutinous cell-block armed with rifles, and one prisoner was shot, but there was little shooting thereafter. Thirty-two men were subsequently charged with riotous conduct and wilful damage. Two of them were also charged with wounding with intent to cause grievous bodily harm. All but ten were sentenced to additional terms of imprisonment.

Soon afterwards, rumours were heard that Dartmoor was to be closed. The Home Secretary, Sir Samuel Hoare, said after a visit to the prison that it was 'strikingly out of keeping with the ideas of prison reform I wish to introduce'. The Dartmoor riot of 1932 remained Britain's most serious prison mutiny for more than forty years, until the riot at Hull in 1976.

Talk of Dartmoor's closure has been around for decades. One writer – a former warder – said in the late thirties that 'this old prison should be closed', and added that the whole place 'shrieks aloud for destruction'. It was regarded as 'condemned and long overdue for demolition' by 1939. It would soon be closed down, it was believed, and the prisoners redistributed about the country. Towards the end of the war, the Prison Officers' Association was told by its chairman at an annual conference that: 'Dartmoor prison is a sink of iniquity not fit for prisoners or staff, and the Home Secretary who closes it will have rendered a service to humanity. The plain truth is that the whole place should be closed and razed to the ground.'

A local historian wrote in the late forties that it seemed probable that 'Dartmoor prison before long will become a thing of the past'. By this time the sentence of 'penal servitude' had been abolished, and there were no longer such things as 'convicts'. But Dartmoor continued to receive prisoners, mostly those sentenced to long terms of imprisonment. James Camb, a ship's steward who had murdered an actress, Gay Gibson, on board a Union Castle liner, was sent to Dartmoor for six months to cool him down after he had caused trouble at Wakefield Prison. He had only escaped the death penalty because capital punishment was under review at the time. John George Haigh also had a spell in

Dartmoor, before he became notorious as the 'Acid Bath Murderer'.

In 1953, a rumour circulated round the prison that the new Queen, on the occasion of her coronation in June, would grant pardons or remissions of sentences to all her subjects who were in prison at the time. The rumour arose, no doubt, from recollections that in 1910, on the accession of George V, remission was granted to all convicted prisoners who had more than a month left to serve on 23 May of that year. Remissions were granted on a pro-rata basis, in accordance with the new King's wish that the prison population should not be excluded from the national rejoicing. Winston Churchill, who was Home Secretary at the time, noted that eleven thousand prisoners had benefited from reduction of their sentences, which amounted in total to five hundred years of imprisonment being struck from the prison population. There was, however, to be no such event in Elizabeth II's time. Dartmoor's governor feared that there might be serious trouble when the rumour was proved false, and he took the precaution of having the whole prison searched with the proverbial fine-tooth comb. Various weapons and rope ladders were found, among other things, and in the end no trouble occurred.

Although only a few men have made escapes from this prison for more than short periods, one who did was Frank Mitchell, the so-called 'Mad Axeman', who was serving a sentence of life imprisonment when he escaped in December 1966, with the aid of the Kray twins. Mitchell was not mad and he had not killed anyone. He had threatened some people with an axe to extort money from them. One day he simply slipped away from an outside working party and was bundled into a waiting car and taken to London.

Earl Mountbatten of Burma had recently been appointed by the Home Secretary, Roy Jenkins, to conduct an enquiry into prison security, following the escape of the spy George Blake from Wormwood Scrubs, and the circumstances of Mitchell's escape were added to Lord Mountbatten's brief. They were startling more for what they revealed about the running of Dartmoor than for the getaway itself. It appeared that he had been indulged by corrupt warders to the extent that he had made shopping trips to Okehampton and visited pubs in the locality.

Later, Mitchell vanished. It was alleged that the Kray brothers had murdered him, because he had become dangerous, threatening to shoot somebody. There was an allegation that Mitchell had been shot and dismembered, but no remains were found, and the Kray brothers were acquitted of his murder. The Krays' own version of the story is that Mitchell was taken from London to Suffolk, and from there to the Continent, and that he is still alive somewhere. After a quarter of a century, Mitchell remains officially on the run from Dartmoor.

There was a widespread belief during the fifties and sixties, both inside the prison and among the general public, that Dartmoor's closure was imminent. Tom Tullett wrote in his book *Inside Dartmoor* in 1966: 'There seems no doubt now that the days of Dartmoor are numbered and that it will close in 1970 . . .' There were slight grounds then for such optimism. But in October 1979, when the local Member of Parliament spoke in the House of Commons about his anxiety over the possible closure of the prison, which would, he said, have 'very serious social implications for Princetown', he was promptly reassured by the Home Secretary, William Whitelaw, that in the prevailing conditions of overcrowding in prisons, 'there is no question of closing down Dartmoor'.

Nearly a quarter of a century later, HMP Princetown, far from being made redundant, has undergone some ominous refurbishment, in the face of yet another recommendation, this time by HM Chief Inspector of

Prisons, that it should be closed down. It is now classified as one of Britain's 'closed central prisons' (others include Parkhurst and Wakefield), where men serving long sentences for murder, violence and sexual offences are held. It seems certain that the most hated of Britain's old prisons will still be there in the twenty-first century – a forbidding grey symbol of nineteenth-century penal ideas, and a depressing monument to human misery and shame.

7

MIDLAND MISERIES

The last quarter of the eighteenth century and the first quarter of the nineteenth brought forth a great surge of prison building in Britain. There were several contributory causes. First, there was a massive increase in urban population in the wake of the Industrial Revolution, resulting in a rapidly growing crime rate in the towns and cities. Second, the notoriously harsh property laws of Georgian Britain had multiplied the list of punishable offences to a countless extent. Third, although the Transportation Act of 1784 allowed the government to send convicts anywhere in the world (with the avowed aim of eliminating the 'criminal class' in this country), the American War of Independence restricted the scope for banishment.

Among this crop of new domestic prisons was the County Gaol at Gloucester, built on the site of Gloucester Castle on the east bank of the Severn, and completed in 1792. Its architects were William Blackburn and, after his death, the county surveyor, John Wheeler, but the important name in connection with Gloucester prison is George Onesiphorus Paul, a wealthy local justice, who organised the building of six new prisons in Gloucestershire, to cope with the new demand created by suspension of transportation to the American colonies.

Paul had the new prison at Gloucester built on the lines of John Howard's penitentiary principles. It was only the second prison to be built with a separate sleeping cell for every prisoner. (The first was at Petworth in Sussex, opened about six years earlier.) There were cells for felons on three storeys, and separate wings for those awaiting trial and those convicted of minor offences. The prison was provided with ample exercise yards. Convicts were to be isolated from society and forbidden access to all except next of kin, who were allowed visits twice a year. Gloucester became the model for prisons built in Britain in the early nineteenth century.

Sir George Paul had to satisfy local scepticism about the wisdom of such reforms. 'I am far from thinking that prisons should be places of comfort,' he assured the doubters. 'They should be places of real terror.' In pursuance of this philosophy, convicts admitted to Gloucester were routinely stripped, searched and medically examined, and then had their heads shaved. Paul advocated the shaving of prisoners' heads partly for hygienic reasons (it was the 'only means of preventing the introduction of vermin to the bedding'), and partly because it was a 'mortification to the offender'. Prisoners were kept in solitary confinement for most of the time, and allowed out for exercise in the yards once a day. They worked in their cells preparing raw wool for local clothiers.

Gloucester prison was soon nicknamed 'the Bastile' (*sic*), and there were internal protests against the regime, one of which, in 1815, resulted in the leaders of the disturbance being given thirty-six lashes each. The first governor resigned, and other prison officers were dismissed because they failed to match up to Paul's expectations in terms of efficiency and self-discipline. The prison also came under attack in the press, notably over the case of a mere boy sentenced to seven years' solitary confinement. Howard had never visualised such a strict regime. The system had to be abandoned in due course because of overcrowding. George Jacob Holyoake was imprisoned at Gloucester for six months in 1842 – the last man to serve a prison sentence in Britain for blasphemy. Holyoake had said during a lecture at

Cheltenham that he did not believe that such a thing as God existed.

The County Gaol at Leicester was designed by the County Surveyor, William Parsons, and built in 1825-8, mainly of red brick, but with a stone entrance gate. This was in medieval fortress style. The gate itself was flanked by round towers and had a false portcullis. This image of strength at once gave the impression that the prison would be very difficult to break *into*. It was intended by this time that prisons should be closed to outsiders, in contrast to the old places like the Fleet and the Marshalsea, but it was hardly necessary for them to have forbidding fortifications. Perhaps the architect was recalling the storming of the Bastille, which had stirred the emotions of the civilised world in his youth.

The prison stands on the south side of the city centre at the junction of Welford Road and Tower Road, close to the Royal Infirmary (built in 1771) and the vast Welford Road Cemetery (opened in 1849), in a sort of eternal triangle of disease, degradation and death. Until public executions were abolished in 1868, patients at the Infirmary were sometimes given the doubtful privilege of watching the hangings outside the prison gates. It is not recorded what effect this macabre shock therapy had on their recovery rate!

William Cobbett stopped in Leicester during his travels in 1830, and had a few words to say about the new prison, and about gaols in general:

> Leicester is a very fine town; spacious streets, fine inns, fine shops, and containing, they say, thirty or forty thousand people. It is well stocked with gaols, of which a new one, in addition to the rest, has just been built, covering three acres of ground! And, as if *proud* of it, the grand portal has little turrets in the castle style, with *embrasures* in miniature on the caps of the turrets. Nothing speaks the want of reflection in the people so much as the self-gratulation which they appear to feel in these edifices in their several

towns. Instead of expressing shame at these indubitable proofs of the horrible increase of misery and of crime, they really boast of these 'improvements', as they call them. Our forefathers built abbeys and priories and churches, and they made such use of them that gaols were nearly unnecessary. We, their sons, have knocked down the abbeys and priories; suffered half the parsonage-houses and churches to pretty nearly tumble down, and make such uses of the remainder that gaols and treadmills and dungeons have now become the most striking edifices in every county in the kingdom.

... But go down into the villages; invited by the spires, rising up amongst the trees in the dells, at scarcely ever more than a mile or two apart; invited by these spires, go down into these villages, view the large, and once the most beautiful, churches; see the parson's house, large, and in the midst of pleasure-gardens; and then look at the miserable sheds in which the labourers reside! Look at these hovels, made of mud and of straw; bits of glass, or of old off-cast windows, without frames or hinges frequently, but merely stuck in the mud wall. Enter them, and look at the bits of chairs or stools; the wretched boards tacked together to serve for a table; the floor of pebble; broken brick, or of the bare ground; look at the thing called a bed; and survey the rags on the backs of the wretched inhabitants; and then wonder if you can that the gaols and dungeons and treadmills increase, and that a standing army and barracks are become the favourite establishments of England!

Twenty years after Cobbett's splendid but ineffectual diatribe, Leicester prison was in the national news, because of its rigorous pursuit of the prevailing dogma that every prison should enforce sentences of imprisonment with hard labour. Leicester had been equipped with the customary treadwheel, which claimed the life of at least one prisoner who was accidentally mangled to death in its machinery. In 1848 Leicester added labour at the crank-wheel to the punishments of all prisoners held there.

The horrors of the treadwheel have already been described (see Coldbath Fields). The crank machine was, if anything, an even worse form of gratuitous cruelty, and was regarded by convicts, with justification, as a 'species of torture'. One of its attractions to prison authorities and staff was that – unlike the treadmill – it could be enforced without letting prisoners out of their cells. Crank labour consisted of winding the handle of an iron drum, which could be screwed tight or weighted to resist turning, sometimes by means of scoops attached to it, like the buckets of a water wheel, picking up heavy sand and dropping it as they reached the top of the drum, only to pick up more at the bottom. The average rate at which the crank could be turned by reasonably fit men was about twelve hundred revolutions per hour. At Coldbath Fields, prisoners were required to do ten thousand revolutions per day, equal to about eight and a quarter hours' labour. Mayhew described the work there as 'very distressing and severe'.

In 1848, the regime at Leicester instituted a system whereby adult male convicts were to achieve at least fourteen thousand revolutions a day, equal to eleven and a half hours' labour, with a system of punishments for failure to meet the regulation workload. Their meals were dependent on performance. The governor, Mr Musson, adopted the Biblical philosophy, 'If a man will not work, neither shall he eat.' The men had to do eighteen hundred revolutions to earn their breakfast; four and a half thousand more for their dinner; and a further five thousand four hundred before supper, leaving two thousand seven hundred to be done in the evening to complete their day's quota. If they did not perform their full tasks, they were not only deprived of their meals, but were subjected to other punishments. They might be flogged, or put in solitary confinement in a dark cell on bread and water, or even confined in straitjackets.

A prisoner named Frederick Holyoake, committed for three months in February 1851 for aiding at a dog fight, had a lacerated hand, and was deprived of his ration of soup and meat, because the prison doctor said that meat would have inflamed his hand. He also sustained a sprained ankle, and was made to keep his foot in cold water for two days, but was not excused his work on the crank.

Soon, the severity of the crank labour and the privation of meals led to numerous cases of a dropsical disease called 'crank oedema', as well as to wasting of flesh, excessive perspiration and deathly pallor. A warder's notebook showed that prisoner C.3.28 (one Goddard), for refusing to work, 'has been without food five days . . .'. Juvenile prisoners were also put to work at the cranks, and were required to achieve twelve thousand revolutions a day. The chief warder, William Godfrey, stated later that the youngest boy he could remember doing crank labour was aged eight.

Meanwhile, one of the new Victorian prisons had been completed at Winson Green, a western suburb of Birmingham. D. R. Hill, the relatively restrained architect of Wandsworth, resorted to the baronial manner when designing the new prison in his home town, and built what Pevsner described as 'a toy fortress, all castellated and round-arched, in red brick with stone dressings, that is hard to take seriously'.

But, serious or not, the authorities at Winson Green prison quickly followed Leicester's example. The governor there was a sadistic former naval officer, William Austin. He had been deputy governor at Tothill Fields in London before coming to Birmingham as deputy to Alexander Maconochie, whom he had displaced after controversy about the latter's humanitarian reforms. Maconochie had come to Birmingham from Norfolk Island, but was dismissed for being too lenient. Under the Austin regime at Birmingham, a boy prisoner, fifteen-year-old Edward Andrews, committed suicide in 1854. Austin ordered even petty offenders to the crank regime in solitary confinement. Those who failed to do the required work were put in straitjackets, drenched with cold water, and thrown into dark cells on bread and water. After two months of these punishments, Edward Andrews hanged himself in his cell.

Austin's harsh methods caused a scandal, and led to the appointment of a committee to enquire into the administration of both Leicester and Birmingham prisons. When the committee's reports were published, they caused widespread shock to an unsuspecting public. The committee learned that thirty-three cells at Leicester had been fitted with crank-labour machines after the enlargement of the prison in 1846. The work demanded by the governor was so severe that no punishment for failure to complete it was bad enough to deter the prisoners from using all possible means to avoid it. The magistrates had been compelled, during the last three years, to resort to corporal punishment far beyond precedent in any other prison in the kingdom.

Musson had worked at Leicester prison for thirty years at the time of the enquiry. His father had been governor there before him, and he had been governor himself for the last ten years. He said that at first crank labour had been confined to 'tramps'.

'Vagrants?' suggested a committee member.

'Vagrants.'

Among the vagrants was one Abraham Lewis, a Jew, who was reported 'absent from chapel' and whipped for being 2,500 revolutions short of his daily grind on the crank. Another was John Henson, a cripple about thirty-six years old, who had been committed for one month for begging. On 21 December 1847, cries were heard from his cell, and he was found with his clothing in flames. He was severely burnt about his upper body, and died the same night. A verdict of accidental death was recorded. Henson had been left in his cell picking oakum, and it was believed he had started the fire by lighting a piece of oakum from the gas light, in order to smoke it.

More common than accidental death, however, was attempted suicide. The committee of enquiry found that attempts at suicide were much more frequent among prisoners subjected to crank labour. Several prisoners who had made such attempts were strapped to the walls of their cells in straitjackets. Among them was Mary Weston, aged twenty-three, who had merely threatened to destroy herself. John Start had extinguished the flame in his cell so that gas leaked into it, and was given three dozen lashes for this and for stealing a piece of bread and walking too slowly during the exercise period. Two suicide attempts had been successful since the introduction of crank labour. William Lambert killed himself by cutting his throat in March 1848, and William Geeson hanged himself in his cell immediately after eating his dinner on 29 March 1853.

The governor was asked by the committee: 'Have you known prisoners in the early period mutilate themselves, or attempt to burn themselves, to avoid the crank?'

'I think there was a case or two,' Musson replied, 'but my mind has not been upon that point at all. I am sorry to say my memory is not very good, and I cannot speak positively.'

'You have no recollection of prisoners being punished for mutilating themselves to avoid the crank?'

'I have no recollection of it.'

Mr Musson had little recollection of anything, in fact, which might be to his discredit.

'Show me the rule of the prison', one committee member said, 'which authorises you to punish an untried prisoner for talking.'

'I do not know what rule there is about it, but ours is upon the separate system; it is an offence to talk.'

The committee found that the prison medical officer, Thomas Benfield, had been required to intervene in 118 cases, within two years, of serious consequences to the health of prisoners resulting from crank labour, and had failed to inform the visiting magistrates; as had the prison chaplain, the Revd William Fox, who repeatedly referred to his failing health as an excuse for not calling attention to the state of the prisoners he saw regularly.

'The system of stoppage of food', the committee reported, 'continued in force from the year 1848 until the month of May 1852, and the evidence before us showed clearly that it had led to results injurious to the health of the prisoners subjected to it, prejudicial to the proper maintenance of prison discipline, and inconsistent, in our judgement, with the legitimate objects of penal imprisonment.'

The governor and chaplain at Leicester were cleared of any charge of cruelty. Most of the blame was laid at the feet of the visiting magistrates, who had, the report concluded, ignored the distinction between 'separate' and 'solitary' confinement, and had used the term 'postponement' of meals to disguise what was, in reality, unlawful deprivation. The governor at Birmingham, Lieutenant Austin, was dismissed and given six months' imprisonment for his abuses of the system.

The authorities at Leicester were asked why the prison had resorted to such severe and unprofitable use of the treadwheel and the crank, when it could have employed prisoners on useful labour in the chief local industry, as had been done at Gloucester, by installing stocking frames. The reasonable answer was that it would have caused a fierce outcry by local knitters against competition by free labour. The Luddite riots were still fresh in the collective memory.

Charles Reade's novel, *It is Never too Late to Mend*, published in 1856, was partly based on reports of these scandals at the prisons in Leicester and Birmingham.

After the abolition of public executions, Gloucester, Leicester and Winson Green all became hanging prisons. Dr J. J. Marshall described an execution he had witnessed at Gloucester in 1886. The victim's name was Hewitt, and the executioner was James Berry:

> I descended immediately into the pit, where I found the pulse beating at the rate of 80 to the minute, the wretched man struggling desperately to (I presume) get his hands and arms free. I came to this conclusion from the intense muscular action in the arms, fore arms and hands, contractions, not continuous but spasmodic, not repeated with regularity but renewed in different directions and with desperation. From these signs I did not anticipate a placid expression on the countenance, and I regret to say my fears were correct, for on removing the white cap (about $1\frac{1}{2}$ minutes after the fall) I found the eyes starting from the sockets, and the tongue protruded; the face exhibiting unmistakable evidence of intense agony.

Leicester was also the scene of a frightful affair in 1911, when the hangman John Ellis prepared to execute William Palmer, who had been found guilty of murdering an elderly widow in a local village. Palmer protested his innocence to the end, and compared his ill-deserved fate with that of Jesus Christ. During his last night in the condemned cell he cried out, 'I'm going to be murdered in the morning!' When Ellis and the officials came to collect him, Palmer leapt at the warders, who fell to the floor with him in a struggling heap. It took four of them to get the violent and cursing prisoner under control and drag him to the gallows.

Among the best-known occupants of the condemned cells in these prisons were Herbert Rowse Armstrong at Gloucester, and Dorothea Waddingham at Birmingham. Armstrong was hanged in 1922 for the murder of his wife Katie, whom he had poisoned with arsenic from a weedkiller. Waddingham was hanged in 1936 for the murder of Ada Baguley, a bedridden inmate of the old people's home she ran at Nottingham.

8

VICTORIAN PRISONS

When Victoria was proclaimed Queen on 21 June 1837, a military hospital at Newport, on the Isle of Wight, was undergoing conversion, and opened in the following year as Parkhurst maximum security prison. Its original buildings dated back to 1799. The first entirely new prison of the Queen's reign was Pentonville, originally called the Model Prison.

Pentonville was only the second prison in Britain to be built by the government instead of by local authorities. The first had been the vast and highly costly Millbank Penitentiary, opened in 1816 but demolished in 1892 as an unsuccessful experiment based on the 'Panopticon' ideas of Jeremy Bentham. (The Tate Gallery now stands on the site.) Epidemics of scurvy and cholera had swept through this prison in the 1820s, and Millbank had had to be evacuated by an Act of Parliament which gave the female prisoners their liberty and sent the male ones to the prison hulks at Woolwich.

Pentonville was built on a site beside the Caledonian Road at Islington, north London. The first stone was laid by the Home Secretary on 10 April 1840, two months after Queen Victoria's marriage to Prince Albert, and the prison was ready for occupation a few days before Christmas 1842. Its architect was Joshua Jebb, an army engineer and first Surveyor General of Prisons, who had converted Parkhurst. He based Pentonville's design on the 'separate system' of the latest American penitentiaries.

Pentonville's eight acres of ground were surrounded by a perimeter wall eighteen feet high. Its five radial blocks of brick, iron and concrete could accommodate five hundred and twenty prisoners. (In 1941 Pentonville suffered a direct hit by a German bomb, which damaged the central part of C Wing. It was never rebuilt. A corridor now links the two undamaged parts, the outer one being called H Wing.) The cell blocks were of three storeys. Every cell was identical, measuring seven feet by thirteen, and nine feet in height. The prison quickly became the model for all new prisons built, not only in Britain, but throughout Europe. Foreign princes and potentates flocked to London to inspect the new buildings and went home to build their own versions. They included the kings of Prussia and Saxony, Grand Duke Michael of Russia and the Archduke of Austria.

Among the new English prisons based on the Pentonville model were Armley Gaol, Leeds, completed in 1847; Wandsworth and Holloway in London, completed in 1849 and 1851 respectively; Winson Green, Birmingham, completed 1850; Walton, Liverpool, completed 1855; and Strangeways, Manchester, completed 1868. (Wormwood Scrubs, London, was built by convicts and completed in 1874, and Brixton, though built originally in 1820, was considerably altered and extended in 1898.) Unlike Joshua Jebb at Pentonville, however, many architects of the subsequent prisons were unable to resist the medieval fortress style of building so castigated by Cobbett. Even Pentonville had an imposing gatehouse with a false portcullis, as a result of Sir Charles Barry, architect of the new Houses of Parliament, being called upon to design the entrance.

Prison gothic sprouted throughout Victorian Britain, with towers and turrets, castellations and machicolations, ramparts and mock portcullises. The prison at Leeds was built by Perkins and Backhouse in what Pevsner called 'the accepted dungeon style'. Holloway was the most flamboyant of the lot – a gothic fortress designed by J. B. Bunning with a castellated and turreted gatehouse and a tower based on the battlemented fourteenth-century Caesar's Tower at Warwick Castle. Liverpool's gatehouse, built of brick with stone dressings, was designed by the Borough Surveyor, John Weightman, complete with mock machicolations and arrow slits.

The 'separate system' was that in which inmates were isolated from their fellow-prisoners at all times, even during services in the prison chapel, where they sat in individual wooden stalls or cubicles, unable to see or communicate with one another. The penal philosophy behind this system was that the walls isolating a convict from other human beings confronted him with his own conscience. John Howard himself had said that 'Solitude and silence are favourable to reflection; and may possibly lead to repentance'. The system's inspiration was the Carthusian priory, or Charterhouse, in which the brethren lived in utter austerity, embracing not only a rule of silence, but almost total isolation. Each monk lived in seclusion in a stone cell, eating, sleeping, studying and praying alone, and meeting his brothers only at church services and on social feast days when they dined together. The spiritual convictions and inner strength of medieval saints, however, were not shared by Victorian sinners.

In Pentonville's earliest years, inmates spent their first eighteen months in solitary confinement. At that stage, prisoners committed to Pentonville were young men with long sentences, carefully selected for their physical fitness to endure hard labour, for they were destined to be transported. No prisoner, said the Home Secretary, 'shall be admitted into Pentonville without the knowledge that it is the portal to the penal colony, and without the certainty that he bids adieu to his connections in England, and that he must henceforth look forward to a life of labour in another hemisphere'. Prisoners went into solitary confinement at Pentonville without any hope of returning to their families and friends. (Later on, some were moved to Dartmoor or Portland as convict labour.)

However tough they may have been physically, many of the men were not strong enough mentally to withstand the long periods of silence and solitude, for no communication was allowed, and when they were let out of their cells for exercise or chapel services, they had to wear face-masks so that no prisoner could enjoy the slight relief of recognising a friend or acquaintance. In June 1843, one John Reeve became the first Pentonville prisoner to be transferred to the Bethlehem Hospital for the Insane (Bedlam), and within eight years, notwithstanding reduction of the period in 'solitary' to twelve months and later to nine, twenty-two prisoners had been declared insane and twenty-six were said to be suffering from delusions, not to mention six who had committed suicide, usually by hanging themselves in their cells.

Experience showed, in other parts of the world as well as in Britain, that the separate system multiplied tenfold the incidence of mental illness among prisoners. Nevertheless, one John Burt was among those who deplored the eventual relaxation in the rigour of the system, saying that it resulted in a 'decrease of moral instruction'. Burt was a Pentonville prison chaplain. Charles Dickens, too, thought prisoners were too well treated at Pentonville, and Thomas Carlyle called the place a 'palace for felons'. The felons included a boy of about fourteen years of age who had been sentenced to four years' penal servitude for stealing a handkerchief worth a shilling.

In the mid-nineteenth century, the severity of the law had made prisoners in just one year, 1849, of one hundred and sixty-seven thousand citizens. The inmates of our prisons around this time included a twenty-five-year-old man named Johnson from Stafford who was given twenty years with hard labour for setting fire to two stacks of straw; a youth of sixteen imprisoned for sleeping in Kensington Gardens; a boy of ten imprisoned for spinning a top; and a girl of eight sentenced to three months for stealing a pair of boots. Henry Mayhew found that in the five years 1851–5, five hundred and thirty-one boys and eleven girls under fourteen were committed to the Tothill Fields House of Correction alone, for periods up to nine months, for stealing goods or money worth less than a shilling.

Those hard men who were able to tolerate the system without succumbing to mental disintegration suffered punishment by the birch and the cat-o'-nine-tails for their insolence or misdemeanours. They might also be confined in dark cells on a punishment diet of bread and water. Here a man might lose as much as five pounds in weight during a confinement of two days. Pentonville was also equipped with crank machines – those grim symbols of nineteenth-century penal philosophy. (Brixton had the doubtful honour of being the first London prison to install a treadwheel.) But by the time the treadmill and crank had been abolished, in 1899, the Prison Commissioners were able to claim that all prison labour was useful work for government departments. This usually meant sewing mailbags, tailoring, shoe-making, and so on.

By 1877, Pentonville had ceased to be a clearing-house for transportees, and accepted all types of prisoners, becoming the chief gaol for shorter-term prisoners in London north of the Thames. Wandsworth was its counterpart south of the river. These prisons also became the chief places of execution in the capital in the first years of the twentieth century. When Newgate was demolished, its scaffold, which was capable of hanging three victims at once, was removed to Pentonville. It was regarded by the hangmen of the time as the best in the country, and on 30 September 1902, William Billington, assisted by Henry Pierrepoint, carried out the first execution in the new location. Early in the following year, the same two men carried out the first execution at Holloway, half a mile away, which had only recently been converted to a women's prison.

The condemned cells at Pentonville and Wandsworth became the last homes of some of Britain's most famous twentieth-century victims of the death penalty. Until the abolition of the death penalty in 1965, Pentonville had two condemned cells flanking the execution chamber in A Wing, this having replaced the Victorian execution shed in a yard. These two London prisons became the scenes of more executions than any other British gaols, Wandsworth holding the record, as well as being the largest prison in the country, with a current official entry of 1,265. Terence and Pauline Morris found in the 1960s that Pentonville was regarded among prisoners as an 'easy nick' compared with Wandsworth. (Pentonville, Wandsworth, Brixton and Wormwood Scrubs between them hold as many prisoners as the total for the five largest provincial prisons – Strangeways, Walton, Winson Green, Armley and Durham.)

One of the first of the new crop of prisons to be completed after Pentonville was that at Reading. The red-brick prison, characteristically battlemented, with towers and bastions, was erected in 1842–4, close to the River Kennet, in Forbury Road, where it still stands. It had one hundred and ninety-two cells for men and twenty-nine for women. Reading prison would have passed through history as just another of Britain's unremarkable small-town gaols, had it not been for the committal there, late in 1895, of a prisoner who made it world famous.

On 25 May 1895, the foreman of a jury at the Central Criminal Court pronounced Oscar Wilde guilty on several charges of immoral conduct, arising from his illegal homosexual practices. The Honourable Mr Justice Wills, after delivering himself of the opinion that the maximum sentence he was allowed to pass was 'totally inadequate for such a case as this', sentenced Wilde to imprisonment for two years with hard labour.

Oscar Wilde, at the height of his success as a playwright, and arguably a man of genius, had already been inside two of Her Majesty's prisons, and was yet to see three more. After his arrest and appearance before a magistrate, he was remanded in custody at Holloway, which had already taken its toll of his mental and physical condition by the time he came to trial at the Old Bailey. During the course of his two trials (the jury in the first having failed to agree on a verdict), Wilde spent some hours in a damp and dirty cell at Newgate, behind the court. After his sentence, he had to spend a further weekend in Newgate before being taken handcuffed in a police van to Pentonville. Here, he was stripped of his clothes and made to get into a filthy bath which had been used by other prisoners before him. Then his hair was cropped by the prison barber and he was given a thorough medical examination, being declared fit for light labour, before dressing in prison uniform, with its broad arrows, and being locked in his cell.

There was never any question of Oscar Wilde being physically unfit to survive imprisonment. He was as strong and healthy as the next man. But he was highly sensitive. It was his mental condition that was under threat. Those who visited him in prison often saw him in tears. Soon there were reports in the newspapers that Oscar Wilde had gone mad and was locked in a padded cell. There was no truth in this, but he did write later of the English prison system that 'The production of insanity is, if not its object, certainly its result . . .'

Wilde was appalled by his cell. He could hardly breathe in it. The prison food was so revolting that he did not eat for several days, and when he did, he suffered from diarrhoea. Nevertheless, he was confined to his cell all night with a tin chamber pot. Wilde, of course, was far from being unique in this respect, and it was not unknown for warders to vomit when they came to unlock and inspect cells in the mornings.

Wilde escaped work at the crank and the treadmill, but had to do several hours of oakum-picking every day. By this time, picking oakum had become a mere punishment with no practical use, like the crank machine, since iron ships had replaced wooden ones. Prisoners had to do the work in solitary confinement, being let out of their cells only for an hour's exercise each day, and the tarred rope gave off a terrible stench in the confined spaces.

R. B. Haldane, the lawyer and Liberal statesman who later became Viscount Haldane, obtained for Wilde – in spite of objections from the prison governor – the privilege of having books and writing materials. Wilde's solicitors, and Lord Alfred Douglas, petitioned Queen Victoria to release Wilde from a sentence that almost everyone agreed was excessively severe. These appeals were refused, and on 4 July 1895, Oscar Wilde, for reasons which are still not clear, was removed from Pentonville to Wandsworth, where he remained for the next six months.

Wilde found Wandsworth worse than Pentonville. The food was 'not fit for dogs', and some of the warders were harsh in their treatment of prisoners. The governor, Captain Helby (a former naval officer), was an advocate of strict disciplinary methods. On one occasion Wilde was caught whispering to a fellow-inmate in the exercise yard, and was punished by being confined in a dark cell for twenty-four hours on bread and water. His spirit broken, he frequently thought of suicide. The prison chaplain, the Revd W. D. Morrison, realised that 'this man would break down long before his sentence came to an end'.

At first, Wilde had resigned himself to the 'plank bed, the coarse fare, the ill-fitting garments, the oakum picking, the monotonous isolation and all the daily humiliations of a prisoner's lot'. But after a few weeks, he had become thin, pallid, and very depressed. His fingers bled and his nails were broken from picking oakum. He was later made to work on sewing mailbags. Despite the hardships, however, Wilde managed to retain his sense of humour. 'If this is the way Queen Victoria treats her convicts', he remarked, 'she doesn't deserve to have any.'

One Sunday morning, Wilde felt so ill that he was unable to get out of his bed, but was warned by the prison doctor that if he did not get up, he would be punished for malingering. He struggled to his feet and got dressed, but fell down and hurt himself, and then collapsed in the chapel. He woke up in the prison hospital with a pain in his right ear, which he had hurt in falling. For some months afterwards, the injured ear bled and ached, developing an abscess which led to a perforated eardrum and partial deafness. When Robert Sherard visited Wilde in the hospital, he reported that Oscar was 'a perfect wreck and says he will be dead before long'. The Home Office became alarmed at the prospect of a public outcry if Wilde were to die in prison or become insane. Two specialists were sent from Broadmoor to examine him. They reported that there was no cause for alarm about his mental health, but recommended that he might be moved to a country prison where he could benefit from outdoor exercise and be given work and privileges more suited to his temperament. In November, Wilde was taken by train to Reading, after standing handcuffed for half an hour on a platform at Clapham Junction, being jeered at by a loathsome mob.

The governor at Reading prison was Major Isaacson, a martinet and despot, who soon declared to one of Oscar's visitors that he was 'knocking the nonsense out of Wilde'. Isaacson was opposed to any of his charges having any books for the first two months of their time in his establishment, and ran the prison, according to Wilde, 'with the greatest harshness and stupidity'. He was very much given to punishments for minor infringements of the rules and particularly, it seems, favoured reductions of diet. In Wilde's case, when later on he had been allowed some books, Isaacson would punish him by taking them away from him. Some warders bullied Wilde, now prisoner C.3.3., but others were more sympathetic towards him.

In July 1896, preparations were being made at Reading prison for the execution of a trooper in the Royal Horse Guards, Charles Thomas Wooldridge, who had killed his wife in a fit of jealousy. Wilde saw the victim at his exercise in the prison yard, and the grave being dug for him in the grounds. He wrote in a letter to Robert Ross that 'the shed in which people are hanged is a little shed with a glass roof, like a photographer's studio on the sands at Margate'. Wooldridge was hanged on 7 July, the hangman being James Billington. When Wilde wrote his *Ballad of Reading Gaol*, after his release almost a year later, it was published with 'C.3.3.' in place of the author's name, and dedicated to 'C.T.W.'

Wilde's physical condition did improve somewhat at Reading. His mental state was a different matter, however. He twice made desperate appeals to the Home Secretary for his early release, fearing that he would be mentally unbalanced for the rest of his life. These appeals were refused. But one result of Wilde's own anxieties, as well as those of his friends, about his mental health was that the Home Secretary gave instructions that he was to be granted writing materials and access to more books. In the meantime, Major Isaacson had been transferred to Lewes, and his replacement at Reading was Major Nelson, a rather more civilised and humane man. Punishments in the prison were cut by half in the new governor's first few months, and Wilde wrote that, although Major Nelson had to observe the rules of the prison system, he knew that they were often 'unjust, stupid and cruel'. Many years later, commenting on Wilde's *Ballad*, Major Nelson said that it was 'not only a faithful description of the effect produced by the hanging of the soldier . . .' but that 'the same dreadful atmosphere of doom affecting warders and prisoners alike, permeates our gaols on the morning of an execution even today'.

Oscar Wilde remarked in one of his permitted letters: 'On November 19th I will have had eighteen months of this black loathsome hell'. He was hopeful that there would be some mitigation of his sentence, but it was not to be. Only convicts under sentence of penal servitude (i.e. three years or more) could earn remission.

Major Nelson made the remaining months of Wilde's imprisonment easier to bear. He was relieved of oakum-picking, and put in charge of the prison library, though he continued to have periods of work in the prison garden, for the sake of fresh air and exercise. His diet was improved, and he was allowed to keep the gas light on in his cell in the evenings so that he could read and write. In January 1897, he began writing the long letter to Lord Alfred Douglas that was eventually published as *De Profundis*. It took him several weeks to compose this bitter and tortured exercise in self-hatred, guilt and almost hysterical recrimination, and he was not allowed to send it from prison, but it was kept and handed to him on the day of his release.

Wilde was very distressed to hear a young prisoner, who was mentally deficient, being flogged. Wilde heard him shrieking and howling as he was given twenty-four lashes, and saw him afterwards, his features disfigured by tears and hysteria. Another source of distress for Wilde was the sight of children in prison. He managed to get three children, imprisoned for poaching rabbits, released from Reading by paying their fines.

There was a new warder, Tom Martin, with whom Wilde made friends during the last two months of his sentence. Warder Martin smuggled copies of the *Daily Chronicle* into Wilde's cell, and did him other small favours. Martin had taken pity on the youngest of these children by giving them biscuits when they had cried with hunger, and when this action was discovered, the child having innocently told a senior warder how kind Martin had been to him, Martin was dismissed. Wilde was moved after his release to write two long and passionately felt letters to the *Daily Chronicle* about this and other miserable affairs, and the need for prison reform in general. But it was not until 1908 that the imprisonment of children was abolished.

Wilde was due for release on 18 May 1897, having served his full sentence. Governor Nelson arranged for him to be taken to London on the previous evening, in order to evade the expected crowd of journalists and the threatened appearance of Lord Queensberry's cronies. The newspapers had announced that Wilde would be taken to Wormwood Scrubs. At least one reported that he was taken to Holloway. In fact he returned to Pentonville, and was set free early the following morning. He died three years later in Paris, aged forty-six, of cerebral meningitis, in agony with a complication of the ear trouble which had been neglected by the prison doctors whom Wilde, whose father was a surgeon, had called 'brutal in manner, coarse in temperament, and utterly indifferent to the health of the prisoners or their comfort'.

At Liverpool's Walton Gaol in January 1910, a prison doctor force-fed Lady Constance Lytton, after her arrest during a suffragette demonstration. The prison staff did not know her identity. She had disguised herself as a working-class woman and called herself Jane Warton.

The doctor offered me the choice of a wooden or steel

gag; he explained elaborately, as he did on most subsequent occasions, that the steel gag would hurt and the wooden one not, and he urged me not to force him to use the steel gag. But I did not speak nor open my mouth, so that after playing about for a moment or two with the wooden one he finally had recourse to the steel. He seemed annoyed at my resistance and he broke into a temper as he plied my teeth with the steel implement. He found that on either side at the back I had false teeth mounted on a bridge which did not take out. The superintending wardress asked if I had any false teeth, if so, that they must be taken out; I made no answer and the process went on. He dug his instrument down on to the sham tooth, it pressed fearfully on the gum. He said if I resisted so much with my teeth, he would have to feed me through the nose. The pain of it was intense and at last I must have given way for he got the gag between my teeth, when he proceeded to turn it much more than necessary until my jaws were fastened wide apart, far more than they could go naturally. Then he put down my throat a tube which seemed to me much too wide and was something like four feet in length. The irritation of the tube was excessive. I choked the moment it touched my throat until it had got down. Then the food was poured in quickly; it made me sick a few seconds after it was down and the action of the sickness made my body and legs double up, but the wardresses instantly pressed back my head and the doctor leant on my knees. The horror of it was more than I can describe. I was sick over the doctor and wardresses, and it seemed a long time before they took the tube out. As the doctor left he gave me a slap on the cheek, not violently, but, as it were, to express his contemptuous disapproval, and he seemed to take for granted that my distress was assumed. At first it seemed such an utterly contemptible thing to have done that I could only laugh in my mind. Then suddenly I saw Jane Warton lying before me, and it seemed as if I were outside of her. She was the most despised, ignorant and helpless prisoner that I had seen. When she had served her time and was out of the prison, no one would believe anything she said, and the doctor when he had fed her by force and tortured her body, struck her on the cheek to show how he despised her! That was Jane Warton, and I had come to help her.

If the Victorian prisons of Britain gradually ceased to be anything like the old medieval hellholes, made so by the severity of their regimes, with flogging, treadmills and all the other horrors, they nevertheless became hellholes for different reasons, more often than not resulting from severe overcrowding, squalor, and the failure of succeeding governments to modernise or replace old buildings. However much Pentonville and its fellow Victorian institutions might have been regarded as the epitomes of advanced penological thinking, light years away from the squalor and chaos of Newgate and the Marshalsea, it was inevitable that they would themselves soon become outdated.

There was a proposal to close Pentonville in 1939, but it survives today as one of Britain's 'general local prisons'. By 1967, it had been assigned more-or-less exclusively to the imprisonment of persistent offenders serving less than a year, and the public was protected from these assorted drunks, vagrants and petty thieves by guard-dogs and closed-circuit security cameras. By 1967 also, corporal punishment in prisons had been abolished. During one year in the previous decade, ten prisoners in different UK establishments had been flogged with the cat-o'-nine-tails, receiving an average of twelve lashes, though two men had each received eighteen lashes.

In 1984, the situation had become so bad in these Victorian buildings, where more than eleven thousand prisoners were living two to a cell and more than four thousand were forced to live three to a cell, that the *Report of Her Majesty's Chief Inspector of Prisons* for that year spelt out some of the revolting details. It described how more than fourteen thousand inmates of the prisons of England and Wales had to use chamber pots to urinate or defecate whilst sharing cells; and that the stench of urine and excrement at slopping-out time caused some prisoners to become constipated, while others 'prefer to use their pants, hurling them and their contents out of the window when morning comes'.

At Brixton, prisoners with severe mental disorders, who should not be in prison at all, have been kept penned up in the appalling F Wing, in conditions which are a disgrace to a country which regards itself as being civilised.

It is hardly surprising that riots have occurred in so many of the old institutions in recent decades, and rooftop demonstrators have become a commonplace of modern life in city suburbs. Smouldering resentments and frustrations, fanned by the stress of overcrowding and squalor, burst into flame and then explode into violence.

The riot that occurred at Strangeways, Manchester, on 1 April 1990 was said to be directed not against the 'screws' and the system, but against one group of prisoners – those charged with or convicted of sexual offences and offences against children. In reality, of course, all prison riots are protests against the system. On the fourth floor of E Wing, rioters terrorised these prisoners – the so-called 'beasts' – by threatening them with death, breaking down the two-hundredweight cell doors with scaffolding poles. Prisoners were beaten up with hammers, iron bars and table legs, and thrown from the gallery into the safety net, where they were bombarded with missiles and showered with urine. One terrified victim slashed his wrists. Another man, whose cell had blood splattered from the floor to five feet up the walls, died two days later. He had been severely beaten up and twice thrown over the gallery rail. Three prisoners were subsequently acquitted of murdering him, because the cause of death could not be identified, beyond any doubt, with his injuries. It had to be said that in one sense this protest was a success. It did not initiate the rebuilding programme which has recently taken place, but it *did* undoubtedly accelerate long-overdue improvements.

Part 2
ISLANDS OF THE DAMNED

INTRODUCTION

When Lord Mountbatten made his recommendations on prison security to the British government in 1966, he wanted a new maximum security prison for what he called Category A prisoners – those whose escape would be highly dangerous to the police or public, or to the security of the state – to be built on the Isle of Wight (of which he was Governor), in addition to those that were already there – the Victorian Parkhurst and the new Camp Hill and Albany prisons. This would have turned the Isle of Wight into a kind of British Alcatraz, and the government rightly rejected the proposal.

Nevertheless, the advantages of the island-as-prison were well established, even in Britain, which had used St Helena, isolated in the South Atlantic, to confine Napoleon Bonaparte for the last six years of his life. There have been persistent rumours that Napoleon was assassinated there. He died at fifty-one, arsenic was found in abnormal quantities in his hair, and he said in his will, 'I die before my time, killed by the English oligarchy and its hired assassins'. But a post-mortem examination showed that Napoleon died of stomach cancer. The British also used St Helena to hold more than two thousand Boer prisoners during the South African war.

At home, Britain has maintained prisons on the so-called Isle of Portland as well as on the Isle of Wight. Drake's Island in Plymouth Sound was once used as a state prison, and adherents of the Parliamentarian cause were confined on it after the restoration of the monarchy in 1660. General John Lambert, who had commanded

Cromwell's army in Scotland, was held on the island for sixteen years until his death in 1684. James Harrington, the political theorist, was also a prisoner there, and is said to have gone temporarily insane as a result. John Lilburne, the pamphleteer and leader of the Levellers, was another who spent some time on Drake's Island.

Islands have long been favoured by governments as ideal sites of prisons and penal settlements, for obvious reasons. They combine the attractions of security and the removal of criminals from the midst of the law-abiding populace. But there are more sinister advantages for the repressive regimes of such hidden-away prisons, too. Hence the idea has a long and notorious pedigree.

ÎLE SAINTE-MARGUERITE
AND CHÂTEAU D'IF

Few nations have exploited the idea of the island prison more than France. Even in Paris, the infamous Conciergerie, where Danton and Robespierre, Marie Antoinette and Charlotte Corday lingered en route for their visits to Madame Guillotine, is on an island in the Seine, the Île de la Cité.

The Atlantic coast islands of Oléron and Ré were used as prisons during the Revolution and long afterwards, the latter especially as a sort of transit camp for those criminals sentenced to transportation.

But two islands in the Mediterranean demand notice here as examples of the horrors of island prisons in Europe. One lies, ironically enough, off that coastline that is now a tourist paradise, the French Riviera. The Île Sainte-Marguerite is the larger of those islands, just offshore at Cannes, known as the Île de Lérines. The fortress on it was built by Cardinal Richelieu, and its high walls and buildings of pale stone have been restored more than once.

The most famous prisoner here was the mysterious so-called 'Man in the Iron Mask', who was confined on the island for ten or eleven years before being moved on to the Bastille in Paris. He was housed in a building erected specially for him, with large windows, and maintained at enormous expense by comparison with the few sous expended daily on other prisoners. The island governor, Monsieur de St Mars, was in the habit of telling curious locals that the mystery man was the son of Oliver Cromwell, or the Emperor of China!

But Sainte-Marguerite is most notorious as a dungeon

for French Protestants after Louis XIV's revocation of the Edict of Nantes in 1685. There is a memorial to six Huguenot pastors who were held here for years in solitary confinement. All except one of them went out of their minds. Nowadays, the island houses a museum devoted to the sufferings of the Huguenots, who were mercilessly persecuted during the reign of the so-called Sun King.

M. de St Mars also had in his charge here for a short time – as well as the Protestants and the masked man – the Italian Count Mattioli, the Duke of Mantua's foreign minister, whom Louis had had kidnapped and imprisoned after discovering that Mattioli had tried to cheat him. The Count was arrested in 1679 and imprisoned at Pignerol. In 1694, he was transferred to Île Sainte-Marguerite. He and other prisoners were marched across the Alps in the depth of winter in a chain-gang. One prisoner died during the journey, and the Count and his valet were both very ill on arrival at the island. Mattioli died soon afterwards.

A later prisoner on Sainte-Marguerite was François Bazaine, Marshal of France, formerly a distinguished soldier who was court-martialled in 1873 for dereliction of duty, after surrendering his entire army of nearly 175,000 men at Metz during the Franco–Prussian war of 1870–1. The surrender helped Bismarck's army to take Paris, by freeing troops who had been engaged in the siege of Metz. Convicted of treason, Bazaine was condemned to death, but the sentence was commuted to twenty years' imprisonment in isolation, and he was brought to this island, when sixty-two years old, to serve his term. The following year he managed to escape, disguised as a woman, and died in Spain fourteen years later.

Just off the coast at Marseilles is a group of three small islands, called Ratonneau, Pomègues and If. The smallest of them, and the closest to the mainland, is If, meaning 'yew'. It is, like the others, an island of white limestone, bearing little vegetation. Francis I built a castle on it in 1524, intending it to form part of the defences of Marseilles, but it was never called into use in battle, and in due course the castle was converted by Richelieu into a state prison for political prisoners, becoming infamous as the Château d'If.

In *The Count of Monte Cristo*, Edmond Dantès, falsely arrested as a Bonapartist agent on the eve of his marriage to his beloved Mercédès, is taken on a boat to an unknown destination until he sees

> within a hundred yards of him the black and frowning rock on which stands the Château d'If. This gloomy fortress, which has for more than three hundred years furnished food for so many wild legends, seemed to Dantès like a scaffold to a malefactor.

Dantès is thrown into a hellish dark and cold dungeon of the castle. The story of his escape, after fourteen long years, by substituting himself for the corpse of his fellow-prisoner, the Abbé Faria, in a sack, with the idea of breaking free before he is buried alive in a grave in the cemetery, is among the world's most imaginative and thrilling prison stories. Dantès finds himself, instead, being thrown from the castle ramparts into the Mediterranean, for 'The sea is the cemetery of Château d'If'. It was undoubtedly Alexandre Dumas Père who made the Château d'If one of the most famous prisons in literature, but the place's notoriety is not confined entirely to romantic fiction.

The pale stone castle's curtain walls were built all along the rocks above the island's shores. Inside these walls were cells built round a central courtyard. These were generally reserved for the more privileged prisoners. Below was a horrifying dungeon, windowless and bare, where they put those prisoners who were never intended to be taken out alive. Few lasted more than a few months in this damp, fetid rat-hole, although one man – a sailor who had struck an officer – lived for thirty years in it, reduced to blindness, deafness and lunacy.

The walls of the Château's cells still, to this day, bear inscriptions made by Huguenot prisoners condemned to the galleys at Toulon and held here during transit. Between 1545 and 1750, some three and a half thousand Huguenots were sentenced to serve hard labour as galley-slaves, and incarcerated here for a time.

Louis XIV, who withdrew the privileges which had been granted to the Huguenots by Henri IV in the Edict of Nantes, held many other prisoners in the Château d'If as well as his Protestant enemies. One of them was the reckless Glandevès de Niozelles, who had the temerity to appear in the King's presence with his hat on, and was sentenced to six years' imprisonment for *lèse-majesté*.

A distinguished prisoner here in later times was Honoré Gabriel Riquetti, Comte de Mirabeau, subsequently one of the great figures of the French Revolution, and a man of 'giant, oaken strength', in the words of Carlyle. But in his youth he was a wild and undisciplined character. After compromising an heiress, Amilie de Marignane, into marrying him, his bride was disowned by her father, and Mirabeau ran up a huge debt of two hundred thousand livres to the tradesmen of Aix-en-Provence. Disowned by his own father, Mirabeau was thrown into prison under a *lettre de cachet*. He was a privileged prisoner, however, because of his rank, and despite the fact that he seduced the governor's wife, he was released after a relatively brief period in a cell that was spacious and tolerably comfortable.

Louis Philippe, Duke d'Orléans, the liberal nobleman who voted for the execution of the King, his brother, during the Revolution, after forfeiting his titles and taking the name 'Philippe Égalité', was sent to the Château d'If when he was suspected of aspiring to the crown himself, and he spent six months there before being returned to Paris and guillotined, for royalism and conspiracy, aged forty-six, in November 1793.

Among the last prisoners of the Château d'If – now a museum which can be visited by boat from Marseilles – were the leaders of the revolution of 1848 against the government of Louis Philippe. They proclaimed the Second Republic in France, but were arrested after its overthrow by Napoleon III's *coup d'état* in 1851. Some of these prisoners died in prison, and there is a memorial to them on the island.

The Château d'If ceased to be used as a prison only in 1872, by which time the government of France was sending its political prisoners to another island, far more remote and even more terrible.

NORFOLK ISLAND

When Captain Cook was exploring the Pacific Ocean during his second voyage, in 1774, he discovered a lonely, cliff-bound and uninhabited island of volcanic origin, about nine hundred miles east of what is now Brisbane, and named it after the Duchess of Norfolk. Its chief attraction to the English at first was that tall pine trees, apparently suitable for the masts of ships, grew in profusion there. But Norfolk Island was soon to become notorious as the worst place in the English-speaking world.

Within little more than a decade after its discovery, the island was colonised by free settlers and convicts transported from the Australian mainland, and became established as a feared penal settlement. One English sailor who saw how prisoners were treated there reckoned it would have been better for them to be hanged than to suffer the flogging, beating and oppression they were subjected to under the regime of the island's governor, Philip Gidley King, a naval lieutenant.

The convicts were employed either in cultivating the land, growing produce that was sent to Sydney, or in stone-breaking to provide material for the island's roads and buildings. The quarry workers spent long hours breaking five cartloads of stone each per day, and if their picks or hammers broke, they were flogged. The officers and soldiers in charge had only contempt for the convicts, and treated them with a degree of cruelty that often amounted to sadism.

The convicts called the place the 'Old Hell'. If a man was sent there for life, the only way of escape, apart from death, was to commit a crime for which he would have to be sent to Sydney for trial. Murder was committed on Norfolk Island simply to earn the killer a trip to the mainland.

For lesser offences convicts were strapped to the 'triangles' and given severe floggings. One man died of heart failure after receiving two hundred and fifty lashes for striking an officer. Many of the convicts were Irish, but the flogger was an Irishman, too – a big fellow whose 'face and clothes usually presented an appearance of a mincemeat chopper, being covered in flesh from the victim's body'. Women convicts were sent to Norfolk Island, too, and lived there in conditions of physical and sexual slavery. They, too, were sometimes flogged.

By early 1814, however, Norfolk Island had been deserted. Its pines had been found, after all, to be unsuitable for ships' spars, and its remoteness made it otherwise uneconomical to run. In 1790, the island had been saved from starvation – after the wreck of a supply ship and the swelling of the population by the ship's crew – only by the slaughter of the island's seabirds – 172,000 petrels – within three months. The island's buildings were demolished, to discourage unauthorised occupation, the domestic livestock killed, and no trace was left of the penal colony for any new visitor to find. The island remained desolate for a decade.

It was reopened as a convict settlement by order of General Sir Thomas Brisbane, appointed Governor of New South Wales in 1821. The first party of convicts of the second settlement – fifty-seven men – was landed on the island in June 1825, to begin the construction of new quarters. Brisbane's successor, Ralph Darling, decided that the place was to be made a place of terror, where the sole aim would be degradation of the most desperate criminals. Under the new regime, no women were to be allowed on the island, and there were to be no free settlers either – only the convicts and their guards.

The years 1825–8 were among the worst in the island's history. It was an 'ugly, brutal and sex-perverted' place. A crime flourished there which would, if described, a visiting bishop wrote, 'make your hair to rise in horror upon the pale flesh'. Homosexuality was endemic among the prisoners, notwithstanding that sodomy was then a capital crime. Young arrivals were routinely raped by the old lags, and a chaplain reported that at night 'the sleeping-wards are very cess-pools of unheard-of vices'. Another witness reported that 'atrocities of the most shocking, odious character are there perpetrated, and unnatural crime is undulged in to excess . . .'

The heart-shaped island, about five miles across from east to west, and closer to New Zealand than to Australia, had its prison settlement, originally called Sydney and then King's Town (eventually corrupted to Kingston), on the southern coast at Sydney Bay, where one of the island's two landing-places was protected by a reef which could be crossed only by whalers rowed hazardously from the ships. The journey to the island from the mainland – which could take two weeks – was itself a horror. Convicts who had already been detained in a prison hulk after being sentenced to a spell on Norfolk Island made the nine-hundred-mile voyage chained together in a dark and filthy prison in the ship's hold.

On the higher ground at Kingston, various houses and administrative buildings were erected in a military formation which became known as 'Quality Row' – they included quarters for clergymen, clerks and storekeepers. Closer to the shore, at Slaughter Bay, prisoners' barracks and a gaol were built. The barracks could accommodate nearly a thousand; the gaol a hundred and thirty. The latter was regarded with dread by convicts. It was begun in 1836, and eleven years later – five years after the completion of Pentonville prison in

London – five cell blocks radiating from a central point were finished. There were two 'dumb cells', which neither light nor sound could penetrate, and which could drive their occupants insane. To the east of the settlement was an ever-expanding cemetery.

Most of the prisoners worked in chain-gangs at the quarry or in making roads, from sunrise to sunset every day, with an hour's break for a meal at midday, their food consisting of cornmeal and salt beef of poor quality. Their number grew to seven hundred by 1834, and to double that number by 1841.

The punishments meted out for crimes and misdemeanours were often sadistic. Prisoners would be given a hundred lashes with the cat-o'-nine-tails merely for saying 'Oh, my God!', or for smiling, or for singing. They were never given medical attention after floggings, and their putrefying flesh was often infested with maggots. Sometimes men who had been flogged would be strapped down in straitjackets to iron bedsteads, so that they could not relieve their bleeding backs and buttocks, and their flesh stank with decomposition.

One witness of the floggings – an Irish curate – reported that 'the ground on which the men stood at the triangles was saturated with human gore as if a bucket of blood had been spilled on it, covering a space three feet in diameter and running out in various directions in little streams two or three feet long'.

A young Irish convict named Frayne, who, after suffering a hundred lashes, told the then-governor, Lieutenant-Colonel Morisset – one of a series of infamous commandants of the prison island – that he was as great a tyrant as Nero, was awarded a hundred more lashes and ordered to be kept in a cell in irons for the rest of his life, and never to be allowed to see daylight again. The second part of this inhuman sentence was not enforced, but Frayne was mercilessly flogged on several occasions, the flagellator himself being threatened with a flogging if he did not inflict the severest punishment on his victim. By the end of each such punishment, the flagellator was as much covered in blood as Frayne, whose only relief from the agony, when he was returned manacled to his cell, was to pour his remaining water ration on the floor and lie on his back in the puddle, which he enlarged by urinating in it.

Another form of punishment involved up to a hundred convicts at a time being made to grind maize by working a crankmill. A witness in 1844 wrote that the labour 'appears to be dreadfully severe; the yells and screams of the unfortunate criminals as they heave at the cumbersome engine almost induces a belief that the spectator is listening to the cries of lost souls'.

Soldiers occasionally tortured convicts by forcing them to stand for hours, naked and in chains, with their bound arms stretched upward. Sometimes a soldier would insert a stick into the cord binding a prisoner's arms and twist it until blood was forced out at the fingertips. The island's blacksmith would deliberately make leg-irons with rough inside surfaces that lacerated the wearer's flesh.

Other tortures included the so-called 'Scavenger's Daughter' – a device whereby a convict was tightly bound by hoops with his head on his knees, and left thus until he fainted with agonising cramps, sometimes after blood had spurted from his mouth, nostrils and anus. There was also the water-pit – a dark subterranean cell where men were confined naked for several days, up to their waists in salt water, unable to sleep for fear of drowning.

Some convicts lay down in their cells at night praying not to wake up in the morning. When thirty men were convicted in 1834 of mutiny, after a failed attempt at escape, fourteen were sentenced to be hanged and the rest to life imprisonment. The sixteen who were condemned to live wept; those who were to die sank to their knees and thanked God that their eternal release was in sight.

Such were the horrors of life on Norfolk Island that every so often convicts would draw lots to choose two men, one of whom was to kill the other in the presence of the rest. The victim would have his release by a quick death that would not, like suicide, consign him to an eternal damnation perhaps even worse than this living hell. The rest – the murderer and the witnesses – would have a brief respite by being sent to the mainland for the trial; and on the mainland there was at least a slim chance of escape. This desperate loophole was closed in 1833 by periodically sending a judge and lawyers to Norfolk Island instead of returning criminals to Sydney to face trial.

Other devices for winning some respite from the horrors of slave labour included inducing sickness by eating poisonous berries, or getting a friend to cut off a toe with a spade or hoe whilst working in the fields. Some men went so far as to blind themselves.

The only governor to bring some humanity to Norfolk Island was Captain Alexander Maconochie, who has been called 'the one and only inspired penal reformer to work in Australia throughout the whole history of transportation'. But he was dismissed from Norfolk Island in 1843, after much reactionary criticism, and returned to England, where in 1849 he was appointed the governor of the new prison at Birmingham. Two years later, he was dismissed from this post too, as being too lenient, and was succeeded by his assistant, Lieutenant Austin, who became notorious for his cruelties. Maconochie was the inventor of the so-called Marks System, in which convicts worked together in groups and had a common responsibility for rewards and punishments. But he was ahead of his time, and it was only in the 1860s that a limited version of his system was introduced into some English prisons.

The last governor of Norfolk Island, who arrived in the summer of 1846, was the most notorious of them all – the Cornishman John Giles Price, model for the brutal commandant 'Frere' in Marcus Clarke's famous novel *For the Term of His Natural Life*. In that year twelve convicts were hanged for their part in a mutiny led by one of them, William Westwood, known as 'Jackey-Jackey', in which four guards were killed. These and the men hanged in the previous mutiny were victims of the largest mass-executions in Australia's history. The second lot were buried outside the cemetery's consecrated ground, in a communal unmarked grave still known as Murderers' Mound.

Norfolk Island was finally abandoned as a convict settlement in 1855, this time because increasing criticism by those who had seen conditions there was making an impression in London. It was thirteen years after transportation from Britain to Australia had ceased, and thirteen years before transportation was completely abolished by the British government. The system had succeeded only in degrading and brutalising subjects of Her Majesty, Queen Victoria – both the convicts and their keepers.

After the last convict had been taken from the island, nearly two hundred residents of Pitcairn Island, thousands of miles away in the Pacific, were shipped to Norfolk Island at their own request and settled there. They were the descendants of the *Bounty* mutineers who, in 1789, had cast adrift Captain Bligh and those loyal to him, and landed at Pitcairn to begin new lives. The surname Christian is still common among the island's population.

Some of the buildings of the former penal colony remain at Kingston. Many of them are in ruins, their stone having been quarried for building by the new populace. The island that Captain Cook referred to as a 'paradise' is now a crime-free place with a permanent community of nearly two thousand, and a thriving tourist industry.

Off the coast of Guyane, or French Guiana, near the town of Kourou, are three small islands – the Îles du Salût, 'Islands of Salvation', so called because some nuns once took refuge there from an epidemic of yellow fever on the mainland, and were saved. The smallest and most northerly of them, and farthest out from the mainland, is the Île du Diable – Devil's Island. The other two islands are called Royale and St Joseph.

The French began using the territory as a penal colony, setting up several settlements on the mainland, at Cayenne, Kourou and St Laurent, and on each of the three islands, commencing transportation when the English were coming close to ending it. The first shipload of convicts arrived in 1852. But Guyane had been used for isolated cases of political exile long before that. During the Revolution, three supporters of the Terror, Bertrand Barère, Jean-Nicholas Billaud-Varenne and Jean-Marie Collot d'Herbois, having turned against Robespierre, were condemned by the National Convention to deportation to Devil's Island. Barère, who had argued for the execution of Louis XVI with the phrase, 'the tree of liberty does not grow if it is not watered with the blood of kings', escaped before being shipped, but was exiled as a regicide after the fall of Napoleon. Billaud-Varenne spent twenty years in Cayenne, refusing the pardon offered by Napoleon, and then took refuge in Santo Domingo, where he died three years later. Collot d'Herbois died in captivity at Cayenne after more than twenty years there.

The unhealthy climate of the region predetermined

that the penal settlements were to have a grim future. Even the civilian population, which did not have to live in the brutal conditions the convicts suffered, was hard put to survive. French attempts to colonise Cayenne were disastrous. Hospitalisation on a vast scale lost the French their working organisation, and ten thousand immigrants died of typhus.

Although neither the harshest nor the most important of the penal settlements, the one that became notorious throughout the civilised world was the Île du Diable – originally the convicts' leper colony until the islands were utilised as a maximum security area. Devil's Island was then reserved almost exclusively for political prisoners, but its name came to be identified in the popular imagination with the whole penal system of French Guiana.

The rejects of French society, *transportés* sentenced to terms of several years, or to exile *en perpétuité*, were shipped out in vessels that left Île de Ré in France twice yearly for St Laurent, via Algeria, where they picked up more convicts. The prisoners were confined in iron cages in the holds of the ships, dark and cold, and allowed one hour of exercise daily, manacled, until those who had not died on board stumbled out into the blinding light and unbearable humidity of tropical Guiana – the ultimate horror of French convicts. Victor Hugo had referred to the place as the 'dry guillotine'. Despair was the common reaction to arrival at the penal settlements.

St Laurent, on the estuary of the River Maroni, was the main and largest camp. Cayenne was reserved for the best-behaved convicts. The islands were largely used for solitary confinement and maximum security. There were various other camps inland, such as Camp Hatte, where disabled prisoners were taken to perfom such work as they were able to do. There were men without limbs; men without hands; men without eyes.

These brutal hellholes had an eighty per cent mortality rate per year, due to disease, murder and suicide. Of those who did not die from illness or brutal treatment, many were kept in harsh conditions for long periods of exile even after their sentences had expired, and most were unable to earn enough for their passages back to France. Those men who *did* return to Europe alive after serving their sentences were often physical wrecks. In the earlier days convicts were made to work naked and in chains in the forests, at the mercy of deadly snakes, mosquitoes, red ants and other insects. They suffered from typhus, malaria and scurvy, tetanus and syphilis. In the space of one year in the time of Napoleon III, more than two thousand Frenchmen died of malaria, dysentery and other diseases. Their only resorts from the torment of seeing untouchable native women in the local villages were through masturbation or the use of *mômes* – the passive homosexuals among them.

Eventually low women were sent out from France to satisfy the needs of the soldiers, who were often former Foreign Legion men, for *their* lives in Guyane were almost as insufferable as those of the convicts they guarded. Many soldiers deserted.

To obtain some temporary respite from their sufferings the convicts would feign madness, or infect or mutilate themselves, to earn spells in hospital. One method was to insert seeds of *Ricinis communis* – the castor oil plant – under the skin, causing alarming swellings. They ran the risks of infection leading to amputation, or blindness, or death. Some prisoners attempted to choke themselves to death by consuming quantities of tobacco. Sometimes soldiers would steal poisons from the medical stores and sell them to convicts who were desperate to commit suicide.

The islands of Royale and St Joseph were reserved for those identified as incorrigibles, and those who had repeatedly attempted to escape from the mainland settlements. Successful escapes were extremely rare. Those who made it became celebrated among the convicts, like the prisoner Dieudonné, who escaped three times. He made his way from St Laurent to Brazil, after having served a period of solitary confinement on Devil's Island. Travelling about ten miles a day through the dense jungle, he made the three-hundred-mile journey only to be extradited by the Brazilian government. On his second attempt, he made it to Venezuela, but was again extradited and severely flogged on his return to St Laurent. But he made yet another attempt, and this time got once again to Brazil, where he was arrested again, but this time extradition was refused, and with the aid of a French journalist, he returned to France and was granted a pardon by the French government.

Devil's Island itself was surrounded by strong currents which made it difficult even for the regular supply vessels to get in and out. St Joseph had quarters for convicts who had become insane, and cells for those sentenced to punishment by silent and solitary confinement, in blocks with the word *Reclusion* painted in large white letters on the outside walls. Because of the shortage of space on the small islands, men who died on them were thrown to the sharks.

In September 1894, a cleaning woman at the German Embassy in Paris found in a waste-paper basket a note, afterwards known as the *bordereau* (memorandum), referring to some items of military information which an anonymous Frenchman was willing to sell to the Germans. Suspicion fell on a Jewish officer on the French General Staff. His name was Alfred Dreyfus.

Arrested and tried for treason by a secret court martial, Dreyfus was convicted by witnesses who were unashamedly anti-Semitic, and by evidence that was sometimes forged. Despite his protestations of innocence, he was sentenced to ritual military degradation and transportation. After being stripped of his insignia in the midst of assembled troops, the former artillery captain was shipped in January 1895 to Guiana. Manacled in an iron cage, he had no idea of his destination until, after a voyage of fifteen days, the ship dropped anchor in the harbour of Île Royale. After spending a month in a cell on this island, isolated from the other prisoners, Dreyfus was transferred to Devil's Island, where he was kept at first in solitary confinement under heavy guard, to 'expiate his abominable crime in merited torments', as Zola was to put it. Dreyfus was Devil's Island's only prisoner at the time, guarded by men on land and sharks at sea. If he should make any attempt to escape, the unequivocal order was to 'blow his brains out'.

Confined to a small hut, where he cooked his own food, he was chained to his bed at night. Disabled from dealing with the insects and vermin which crawled over him during the hot nights, he suffered the tortures of swellings and sores, and drew blood copiously whenever he was able to scratch his tormented flesh. He caught malaria, suffered from chronic dysentery, and experienced ghastly nightmares. Later, he spent much of his time sitting on the cliffs at the island's northern tip, gazing out at the vast Atlantic Ocean that separated him from his native land and the family he might never see again.

Whilst Captain Dreyfus was thus incarcerated, it became clear in France that the spying of which he had been convicted was still going on, and a campaign was mounted to free him. But when a counter-espionage officer suggested to his superior that a mistake had been made, the general's response was: 'If you keep silent, no one need know.' Few people, he thought, were going to worry about a Jew thousands of miles away on the Île de Diable. It was an error of judgement. The officer who had raised the matter, Lieutenant-Colonel Picquart, did not keep silent. He became convinced that the real spy

The confined exercise yard at Newgate, by Gustave Dore.

Oakum Picking at Coldbath Fields Prison, London.

HMS *York* in use as a prison hulk at Portsmouth 1828.

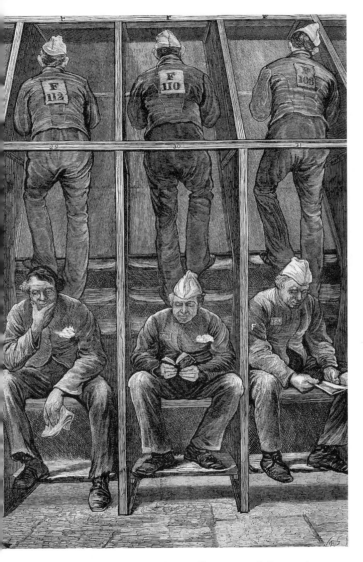

The Treadwheel at Clerkenwell House of Correction,
London. (Mansell Collection)

Russian convicts in transit to Siberian prison camps.
(Mary Evans)

(*opposite page*)
French Prisoners being transported to Guyana in 1903.
(Mary Evans)

Alcatraz – the much mythologised prison island in San Francisco Bay, California. (Associated Press/Topham)

The 'Man in the Iron Mask' in the Bastille, Paris. (Mary Evans)

The storming of the Bastille. (Mansell Collection)

The Lubyanka, Moscow, with the statue of 'Iron Felix', now demolished. (Associated Press/Topham)

WARNING - DANGER
DO NOT APPROACH THIS FENCE.
GUARDS HAVE ORDERS TO SHOOT.
BY ORDER
ACHTUNG
BERÜHREN DES ZAUNES VERBOTEN
WACHEN HABEN BEFEHL ZU SCHIESSEN

Spandau Prison, Berlin, now demolished. (Associated Press/Topham)

was a Major Esterhazy, but Picquart was dismissed from his post for voicing his suspicions. Esterhazy then demanded a court martial in order to clear his name, and this being granted, he was promptly acquitted. People in the streets cheered and shouted, 'Death to the Jews!' France was divided by the *cause célèbre*, the participants becoming known as 'Dreyfusards' and 'Anti-Dreyfusards'.

At this point a powerful new voice was heard in defence of Dreyfus – that of the novelist Emile Zola. He wrote an open letter to the President of France in *L'Aurore*, whose editor was Georges Clemenceau. Zola's piece, entitled *J'accuse*, denounced the court martial of Esterhazy as an army cover-up. It caused a sensation, and Zola was charged with libel. In his long speech, supposedly in his own defence, the fearless Zola returned to the attack:

> Dreyfus is innocent. I swear it! I stake my life on it – my honour! At this solemn moment, in the presence of this tribunal, which is the representative of human justice: before you, gentlemen, who are the very incarnation of the country, before the whole of France, before the whole world, I swear that Dreyfus is innocent. By my forty years of work, by the authority that this toil may have given me, I swear that Dreyfus is innocent. By the name I have made for myself, by my works which have helped in the expansion of French literature, I swear that Dreyfus is innocent. May all that melt away, may my works perish, if Dreyfus is not innocent! He *is* innocent.

Nevertheless, Zola was found guilty, and sentenced to a large fine and a year's imprisonment. After the failure of his appeal, he fled to England, where he continued his campaign. Another writer who came to the defence of Dreyfus was Anatole France, who later satirised the affair in his novel *Penguin Island*.

After protracted investigations and nationwide controversy, it was at last decided that the conviction of Dreyfus must be annulled, and a retrial was ordered. In the summer of 1899, after four long years which had turned his hair grey, Alfred Dreyfus was brought from Devil's Island back to France. He was now bearded, and the strain of his banishment had made him look much older than his thirty-nine years. To the astonishment and outrage of every fair-minded person in France and abroad, the retrial again found Dreyfus guilty, and sentenced him to ten years' imprisonment. This was clearly a feeble attempt by the army at damage limitation, and ten days later, President Loubet announced a free pardon for Dreyfus. The guilty Esterhazy had already fled the country. He lived for a time at Harpenden, in Hertfordshire, earning his living as a salesman of tinned food.

Seven years afterwards, in 1906, Dreyfus was fully exonerated and his army commission restored. His greatest champion, Zola, had been found dead at his home the day after he had returned to Paris in 1902. It was suspected by some that his chimney had been blocked deliberately by Anti-Dreyfusards to cause his death by carbon monoxide poisoning. Other political prisoners followed Dreyfus to Devil's Island, and during the First World War France sent its traitors and deserters there.

The death penalty for capital offences in Guiana was administered by guillotine, as a rule, but there were exceptions. When a young Frenchman named Brock, who was serving thirty years for burglary, was sentenced to death at St Laurent for killing one of the guards, some of the other convicts envied him his release from this living hell, but not when they heard what had happened to him. He had been taken into the jungle, manacled to a tree and left to the mercy of the burning sun, thirst, hunger and poisonous snakes and insects, until he died two days later. One of Brock's executioners – a prisoner granted privileges for doing the job – had eventually walked into the jungle and cut his own throat.

The terrible privations suffered by convicts in Guyane made it almost axiomatic that their minds dwelt constantly on the idea of escape, but only a few succeeded in getting away. The old lags carried about with them small cylindrical capsules, made of aluminium or other metal, in which they kept the small amounts of money they had managed to secrete. These *plans*, as they were called, were inserted in their rectums, the only places safe from discovery by guards, or theft by fellow convicts. They had to be constantly on guard against *mouchards*, convicts who had been granted certain privileges to act as stool-pigeons and help to foil escape attempts.

Those who attempted to escape overland often died after getting lost in the jungle. They were also in danger of being killed and eaten by the native tribes. Those escapees who left by sea, after making rafts or buying canoes from natives with the money in their *plans*, often drowned, or were swept ashore by the Atlantic currents. Their aim was always to reach a country, such as Venezuela, which had no extradition treaty with France, but so many were wrecked on the marshy coast of Surinam that the area near Nieue Nickery was known to the Dutch as the 'Frenchman's grave'. Pierre Bougrat, a doctor, was one of a number of prisoners who escaped from the mainland. He had been sentenced to hard labour for life, being convicted of the murder in Marseilles of a friend and patient of his, Jacques Rumebe, from whom he had stolen twenty-five thousand francs. Bougrat escaped to Venezuela in 1927, and spent the rest of his life there. Robert Vernon, however, who also escaped from Guyane in the same year, having been convicted of robbery with violence, went back ten years later, with a sentence of twenty years, after being found guilty in Paris of the murder of a crook named

Max Cassell in London, and dumping his body in a lane near St Albans.

Another of the Île du Diable's famous, if fairly brief, residents was Henry Charrière, better known by his nickname, Papillon – 'butterfly'. Charrière was convicted at the age of twenty-five of the murder of a pimp and police-informer in Paris, and was sentenced to transportation for life to French Guiana. Charrière, protesting his innocence, swore that he would not serve the sentence, and he became expert at escaping from the toughest security prisons the French could devise.

After escaping from the mainland settlement, and enjoying several months of freedom before his recapture, he was sentenced to two years' solitary confinement on St Joseph. Then he was sent to Royale, and went back and forth between these two islands for one reason or another until, in 1941, he was sent to Devil's Island, where there was a block for ten ordinary convicts in addition to the huts with corrugated-iron roofs where the political prisoners lived. Charrière became determined to escape from there or die in the attempt.

Convicts on the escape-proof Devil's Island had a considerable amount of freedom, and Papillon spent much of his time fishing and studying the actions of the Atlantic waves breaking on the rocks. Experimenting with sacks of coconuts, he found that a large wave crashing on the headland at high tide would carry a floating body so far out to sea, as it receded, that the succeeding smaller waves would not drive it back again.

It was a Sunday evening when Charrière and a fellow convict threw themselves into the ocean, each strapped to a makeshift raft consisting of two sacks of coconuts bound together. The huge wave they had waited for swept them three hundred yards out to sea, and they then allowed the tides to carry them northward to the mainland coast. When they reached the shore, after forty hours at sea, Charrière's companion was sucked beneath the mud, but Papillon made his way into the jungle, and finally won his permanent freedom in Venezuela, twelve years after leaving Paris as a convict.

In the 1930s, increasingly bad publicity about the terrible conditions in the penal colonies eventually led the French government, by a decree of June 1938, to abolish transportation. It was not until 1953, however, that the last prisoner was finally repatriated. In the eighty-six years of Guyane's penal history from 1852, more than seventy thousand convicts had been imprisoned there.

France is now promoting its Overseas Department of Guyane as a tourist area, and some relics of the convict settlements can still be seen, although squatters have largely taken over the chief mainland settlement at St Laurent on the estuary of the Maroni River. The museum at Cayenne has paintings of convict life. There are grim reminders on the Îles du Salut, such as various former prison buildings on Île Royale and the warders' cemetery on Île St Joseph, but visits to Devil's Island are still restricted by the difficulty of landing boats there.

4
SAKHALIN

In the mid-nineteenth century, the Tsar of Russia, Nicholas I, established a penal settlement on the large island of Sakhalin, off the eastern coast of Siberia in the Sea of Okhotsk. The long, narrow island is almost as close to the northern Japanese island of Hokkaido, across La Perouse Strait, as it is to the mainland of Russia. After being administered jointly with Japan for more than twenty years, the cold and sunless island of mountains, tundra and conifer and birch forest passed entirely to Russia in 1875, and the island was maintained as a state prison settlement by Alexander II and III. (Sakhalin passed to Japan after the Russian Revolution, and was only recovered wholly by the Soviet Union at the end of the Second World War.) The site of the first Russian prison camp in 1857 was at Dué, the most forbidding of the island's penal settlements. Sakhalin was the Russian equivalent of Devil's Island, and in the horrors of existence there, it anticipated Stalin's notorious Gulag camps. There was a story that when the Russians first arrived on the island, the shaman of the aboriginal Gilyaks cursed Sakhalin, and predicted that no good would ever come of it.

In 1890, Anton Chekhov went to study the conditions in which the convicts of Tsar Alexander III lived. The young doctor set out from Moscow in April to cross the hazardous five thousand miles through Siberia, reaching the island in mid-July. He landed with a new contingent of convicts at the capital, Aleksandrovsky Post, a small town of wooden cabins. Chekhov soon met the Governor-General of the island, Baron Korf, who told him he was convinced that the prisoners on Sakhalin lived better than in any other place in Russia or even in Europe.

Chekhov described the convict life of Sakhalin in a factual and analytical manner forty years after Dostoevsky had recalled in *Memoirs from the House of the Dead*, thinly disguised as a novel, his experiences as a convict serving four years' hard labour in a military prison at Omsk, in western Siberia. There he had been threatened with a flogging almost immediately on arrival, by the assistant commandant, Major Krivtsov, whom Dostoevsky referred to in his letters as a 'thorough-going bastard, this primitive, niggling, drunken mediocrity . . .'

I have seen many convicts who had been frequently and cruelly whipped, but I do not remember one of them uttering a groan. After such an experience, however, the countenance is pale and distorted, the eyes glitter, the look wanders, and the lips tremble so that a patient sometimes bites them till they bleed.

The soldier who had just come in was twenty-three years of age. He was a well-built and rather fine-looking man, tall, splendidly proportioned, with a bronzed skin. His back, uncovered down to the waist, was terribly lacerated, and his body now trembled with fever beneath the damp sheet with which his back was covered. For about an hour and a half he did nothing but walk up and down the room. I watched his face: he seemed to be thinking of nothing; his eyes had a strange expression, at once wild and timid; they seemed to fix themselves with difficulty on the various objects. I fancied I saw him looking attentively at my hot tea; the steam was rising from the full cup, and the poor devil was shivering and clattering his teeth. I invited him to have some; he turned towards me without saying a word, and taking the cup, swallowed the tea at one gulp without adding sugar. He tried not to look at me, and when he had finished he returned the cup in silence without making a sign, and then began pacing up and down as before. He was in too much pain to think of speaking to me or thanking me. As for the other prisoners, they refrained from questioning him; when once they had applied compresses they paid no more attention to him, thinking, probably, that it would be better to leave him alone and not worry him with their questions or their sympathy. The soldier seemed quite satisfied with this arrangement.

Dostoevsky also anticipated Chekhov in another concern:

For many years I was unable to understand a certain fact which plagued me like an insoluble problem. I must speak of it before continuing my narrative. I am thinking of the chains which every convict is obliged to wear, however ill he may be; even consumptives have died beneath my eyes, their legs weighed down with irons.

Everybody was accustomed to it and regarded it as an inevitable fact. I do not think the doctors themselves would have thought of demanding the removal of the irons from convicts who were seriously ill, not even from the consumptives. The chains, it is true, were not extraordinarily heavy; they did not in general weigh more than eight or ten pounds, which is an endurable burden for a man in good health. I have been told, however, that after some years the legs of the convicts dry up and waste away. I do not know whether that is true. I am inclined to think it is; for the weight, however light it may be (say not more than ten pounds), if it is permanently fixed to the leg, increases the weight of the limb abnormally, and at the end of a certain time must have a disastrous effect on its development.

The danger to a healthy convict is not so great, but the same cannot be said of the sick. For those who were seriously ill, for the consumptives, whose arms and legs dry up of themselves, this additional burden is insupportable. Even if the medical authorities claimed exemption for the consumptive patients only, I am certain that it would prove an immense benefit. I shall be told that convicts are malefactors, unworthy of compassion; but ought we to show increased severity towards those on which the hand of God already weighs? No one will believe that the object of this aggravation is to reform the criminal, and after all, the consumptive prisoners are exempted by the courts from corporal punishment.

There must be some mysterious and important reason for the present system, but what it is, it is impossible to understand. No one believes – indeed, one cannot believe – that a consumptive man will run away. Who could even imagine such a thing, especially if the disease has reached a certain point? It is impossible to deceive the doctors and lead them to mistake a convict in good health for a consumptive, for this particular malady can be recognised at a glance. Do irons help to prevent a sick convict from escaping? Not in the least. The irons are degrading and shameful, a physical and moral burden; but they will not hinder a man attempting to escape. The most awkward and least intelligent convict can saw through them, or break the rivets by hammering at them with a stone. Chains, then, are a useless precaution, and if they are worn as a punishment, should not that punishment be spared to dying men?

Dostoevsky wrote that the people in Russia who showed most compassion for convicts were doctors, and Dr Chekhov showed his compassion in the book he wrote after visiting Sakhalin.

The convicts of Sakhalin were all condemned, in effect, to banishment for life, for even when they had served their sentences for the crimes they had committed, they had to remain in exile, either on the island or on the Siberian mainland, as settlers, and could never return to European Russia. Living in damp and stinking huts all over the island, with half of their heads shaved, so that they were instantly recognisable even if wearing respectable clothes, or no clothes at all, they worked in chaingangs, mining coal, felling timber, or labouring at agriculture and road-building. In France, chain-gangs of convicts, shuffling along in their clanking shackles, became public spectacles second only in their mass appeal to the ritual of public executions. Here on this remote island, they were taken for granted. Some prisoners were chained to wheelbarrows whilst working in the mines on their stomachs. Escape attempts were not uncommon, but those who managed to reach the mainland were faced with the prospect of crossing the Siberian wasteland, and many of those who were not recaptured quickly were eventually found dead.

The chief convict settlements on Sakhalin were at Aleksandrovsk, Dué and Voyevodsk, and Korsakov in the extreme south of the island. The conditions the prisoners lived in were appalling. At Aleksandrovsk Chekhov described the

> rattling of a huge, awkward padlock, certainly bought from an antique dealer, and we enter a small cell where at present twenty men are incarcerated. They have recently been caught attempting to escape. They are bedraggled, unwashed, in chains, in hideous foot coverings made of rags and rope. One half of their heads displays a dishevelled mass of hair; the other half is shaven, and already the hair is beginning to sprout. All are emaciated and shabby, but their gaze is courageous.
>
> There is no bedding. They sleep on the bare floor. In the corner stands a chamber pot. Each prisoner must take care of his natural needs in the presence of twenty witnesses. One begs to be released and vows he will never again attempt to escape. Another begs to have his irons removed. A third complains that he does not get enough bread.

Chekhov saw men in communal cells using wet clothing for bedding on their plank beds, and lying in underwear 'saturated with excretions' from their bodies. Neither the men nor their clothing had been washed for a long time, and they were full of lice. They habitually squashed bugs on their plank beds with their fingers, and the air was foul and fetid. 'The prison soup looks like a semi-liquid porridge made of groats and potatoes cooked to a pulp, with little red pieces of meat or fish floating in it. Some of the officials praise it, but they do not dare to eat it themselves.'

Convicts were susceptible to a great variety of diseases – pneumonia, typhoid fever, scurvy and syphilis – but the most common cause of death was tuberculosis, which Chekhov ascribed to the living conditions and the oppressiveness of penal labour. Nearly half of all deaths from tuberculosis were in the 22–35 age group – workers in the prime of life.

Unnatural deaths were common, too. Execution and suicide accounted for most of these, but there were cases of men being frozen to death, drowned, or crushed by falling trees, and one man was torn apart by a bear.

The women on Sakhalin were heavily outnumbered by men, and there was a great deal of prostitution on the island. The need for prostitutes was so great that neither old age nor extreme youth, nor ugliness, nor even tertiary syphilis were regarded as impediments. Aleksandrovsky Post was well known for its brothels. Female convicts, brutalised by transportation, often went into the 'harems' run by prison warders and local officials. But the free women on the island – wives who had come voluntarily as settlers to be with their banished husbands – often turned to prostitution, too. Chekhov met a sixteen-year-old girl who had become a prostitute at the age of nine, and one free woman ran a brothel populated with her own daughters. Chekhov also came across a Polish convict carpenter, living with his mistress 'who, they tell me, gave birth at twelve years of age having been raped by some prisoner. . .' . The Europeans brought syphilis to the native population.

There were barbaric punishments for serious offences such as murder and attempting to escape.

Punishments which humiliate the offender, embitter him and contribute to his moral degradation, those punishments which have long since been regarded as intolerable among free men, are still being used here against settlers and convicts. It is as though exiles were less subject to the dangers of becoming bitter and callous, and losing their human dignity. Birch rods, whips, chains, iron balls, punishments which shame the victim and cause pain and torment to his body, are used extensively. Floggings with birch rods and whips are habitual for all kinds of transgressions, whether small or large.

Chekhov suffered from nightmares after seeing a convict flogged with a thonged whip at Dué. The wretch, whose name was Mylnikov, had been sentenced to ninety lashes for murdering a Cossack and his two grandchildren. After being fastened by his hands and feet to a sloping bench, he shrieked and vomited as the skin peeled from his naked body under the blows and his back turned into a raw swollen mass of crimson and bleeding flesh. The executioner who administered this punishment was a man named Tolstykh, who had been sentenced to penal servitude for hacking off his wife's head.

Dué was the former capital of penal servitude on the island. 'In the cells I saw a vagrant who had chopped off two of his fingers. The wounds were wrapped in a filthy rag.' Voyevodsk was reserved for the most infamous criminals, who were kept shackled with balls and chains. Chekhov reported that at places such as Voyevodsk and Derbinskoye, he had seen the ultimate in human degradation. He spent three months on Sakhalin, and called it a hell. The result of his expedition was his longest work, *Sakhalin Island*, in which he gave an account of prison conditions which rivals in thoroughness and objectivity the work of John Howard. He wrote to his friend Suvorin:

Except for Australia in the past and Cayenne, Sakhalin is the only place where the use of convicts for colonisation can be studied . . . we have let *millions* of people rot in jails, we have let them rot to no purpose, unthinkingly and barbarously. We have driven people through the cold, in chains, across tens of thousands of versts, we have infected them with syphilis, debauched them, bred criminals, and blamed it all on red-nosed prison wardens. Now all educated Europe knows that we, not the wardens, are to blame . . .

5

ROBBEN ISLAND

Robben Island, a tiny island compared with Sakhalin, lies seven miles off Cape Town in Table Bay. The island is a bleak and treeless rock frequently bombarded by rough winds and stormy seas; cold, dank and often enveloped in thick fog in winter. Inhabited by rats and venomous snakes, and patrolled by sharks, Robben Island became the cradle of European colonisation of South Africa in the seventeenth century, when convicts from Newgate were landed on it. Britain was toying with the idea of the Cape as a suitable place for transportation, before it settled on Botany Bay.

The Dutch East India Company first established a formal prison on the island, but the British used it, too, for housing a leper colony and the incurably insane, as well as criminals of all races – a classic instance of the use of an island for putting polite society's undesirables out of sight and out of mind. One visitor described the place as 'one of the bleakest and most wretched spots on the face of the earth'.

Early convicts were often flogged and branded, and made to work at crushing and burning seashells for lime. Eventually a whaling station was established on the island.

Few prisoners ever escaped from Robben Island. A Xhosa chief known as Makanda surrendered to the British after a failed attack on Grahamstown in 1819. He was sentenced to life imprisonment and sent to the island, and attempted to escape in the following year by swimming to the mainland, but was drowned.

In 1857 another Xhosa leader, Maqoma, was among six prisoners who had been sentenced to death but had their sentences commuted to twenty years' hard labour on Robben Island. Maqoma had been sentenced by a kangaroo court for various alleged crimes, and taken to Cape Town in chains. The Xhosa people, starved of land, were slaughtering their own cattle in the belief that this would lead to the resurrection of their warrior ancestors, who would drive the white men into the sea. On Robben Island, Maqoma was excused hard labour on account of his advanced age, and he was one of the few convicts ever allowed to have his wife with him on the island. They lived in a hut at the abandoned whaling station until 1869, when Maqoma was released by order of the new governor of Cape Colony, Sir Philip Wodehouse. But two and a half years later, Maqoma was arrested again on the mainland and sent back by a local magistrate without charge or trial. He died in 1873, an old man and tribal chieftain who was buried on the island without ceremony in an umarked grave.

In the early 1960s, the South African Minister of Justice, B. J. Vorster, made Robben Island a maximum security prison for non-whites, and it soon became the most dreaded of South Africa's many prisons. (White political prisoners, such as Denis Goldberg, who was sentenced to life imprisonment in 1964, were usually held in the Central Prison in Pretoria. Goldberg spent twenty-one years there.) It took three-quarters of an hour to reach the island by ferry from the mainland. The prison's isolation was increased by an order that no ships were to sail within a mile of the island's shores. The majority of its inmates since that time have been Asian and black African prisoners (male only) incarcerated for political offences.

Prisoners themselves built much of the modern prison, including an eight-cell isolation block surrounded by a thirty-foot wall which separated the political prisoners from the criminals serving life sentences. It was a grotesque punishment designed to reduce morale – black Africans forced to construct part of the apparatus of apartheid.

The prison is a place of stone and brick buildings and barred windows, with high wire fences and walls surmounted by barbed wire. There is a gateway with the name 'Robbeneiland' above, ironically flanked with the word 'Welcome' in English and Afrikaans. The prisoners also quarried the island's stone for building work in Cape Town and elsewhere, chained together by their ankles in the limestone quarry to carry out this backbreaking work with picks and shovels, often under the burning sun and always under the supervision of tough and sometimes brutal warders, who would beat up prisoners for no apparent reason. Alsatian and Rottweiler dogs accompanied the guards, one of whom had a swastika tattooed on his hand. Prisoners were not allowed to communicate with one another, and were deprived of food if caught talking. They had virtually no contact with the outside world. They were permitted to receive one letter and one half-hour visit every six months, but because of the difficulties of reaching the island from places as distant as Johannesburg, some prisoners spent many years of their lives here without ever receiving a visitor. Visitors were separated from prisoners by a thick glass partition, and could only communicate by telephone. Letters they wrote were limited to five hundred words and were heavily censored.

Robben Island's most famous prisoner was officially No. 466/64, known among his friends on the island by his clan name, Madiba. Nelson Mandela spent nearly twenty years on Robben Island, and at first was locked up all day, with no opportunity for exercise, in a seven-foot-square cell lit by one forty-watt bulb. He slept on a mat on the floor, and was inadequately fed. After three months of solitary confinement, he had lost nearly forty pounds in weight, and his appearance was affected by prison pallor. Later, he was allowed to work at stone-breaking in the prison yard, and in the limestone quarry.

Walter Sisulu (Secretary-General of the African National Congress) also became a prisoner on the island in 1964. But the mass exile of alleged subversives by the South African government proved counter-productive. Robben Island became known among black prisoners as 'Mandela University', because ANC veterans took full advantage of their unique opportunity to educate younger prisoners in black African politics, so that they could spread the message on the mainland when they were released. In April 1982, Mandela, Sisulu and others were transferred to Pollsmoor maximum security prison on the mainland.

Typical of the treatment to be expected from the authorities by imprisoned black activists were the cases of two student leaders, Wantu Zenzile and Siphiwe Mtimkhulu, who were detained and tortured in the early 1980s. Zenzile, in his early twenties, sustained permanent damage to his ears through severe torture. Mtimkhulu was paralysed with thallium, an illegal substance administered to him in prison, and he vanished without trace in 1982.

Characteristic of Robben Island's prisoners under the system of apartheid was Ebrahim Ismael Ebrahim, an Indian Muslim who was sentenced in 1964 to fifteen years on Robben Island for sabotage. Released after serving his full term, in 1979, he was kidnapped by South African police in Swaziland, where he had been forced into exile, and sentenced, as a senior ANC official, to a further twenty years' imprisonment for treason, after being tortured. He was released from the island in 1991, aged fifty-four, with only one hour's notice. He had spent twenty-two years of his life in the island prison.

Bill Nair was another activist who spent twenty years on the island, and many more spent periods of ten years there, such as Jacob Zuma, who was sentenced in 1963, when he was twenty. Nair and Zuma were both members of Umkhonto we Sizwe, the military wing of the African National Congress.

It will be interesting to see what happens to Robben Island in the new democratic republic, now that black South Africans have a voice in government. Few of them, presumably, want to perpetuate as a place of incarceration this island which has been the scene of isolation and suffering for so many of their ancestors for more than three centuries.

6

ALCATRAZ

Alcatraz is an island in San Francisco Bay, California, lying east of the Golden Gate Bridge. It was so named by the Spaniards – Isla de Los Alcatraces – after the clouds of pelicans which surrounded the island when they discovered it in 1775. It became a military fortress, and was first used as a prison temporarily in 1906, on loan from the army, when the San Francisco earthquake threatened the safety of the city's jails. The army built the first cell-block, as well as roads and other buildings, using army prisoners sentenced to hard labour. The cell-block was completed in 1912 and had a capacity of six hundred. The island had its own lighthouse.

Alcatraz was used as a disciplinary barracks during the First World War, but afterwards fell into disuse. Then, in 1933, after a series of well-publicised US prison escapes during the gangster era of the late twenties and early thirties, the island was transferred to the Federal Bureau of Prisons and converted into a maximum security prison for incorrigible convicts – a formidable fortress of steel and concrete on foundations of granite. It became commonly known in the American underworld as 'the Rock'. The new prison could accommodate three hundred and two, but it was never filled to capacity. The average population of Alcatraz was two hundred and sixty.

The prison's central building, with its three-tier main cell-block, kitchen and mess hall, stood in a large yard surrounded by high walls well protected by barbed wire. Overlooking the yard was a catwalk which was constantly paraded by guards armed with sub-machine-guns, rifles, tear-gas guns and revolvers. At first there were old army cells deep underground which were used as dungeons for solitary confinement in darkness, but this was stopped in 1939 when a San Francisco judge declared their use a cruel form of punishment, and unconstitutional. D Block was henceforth used as an isolation block for solitary confinement. Disruptive inmates were confined in steel cells for up to three days in total darkness. Alcatraz had automatic locks, electric eyes and – in the mess hall – tear-gas bombs suspended from the ceiling. Only forks and spoons were allowed in the mess hall, but convicts worked out ways of shaping various items into knives that were used in violent attacks on other prisoners. The small individual cells, five foot by nine, each contained a table, a sink and a lavatory, as well as a bed. There were workshops where prisoners, who wore blue shirts, were employed in constructive occupations such as book-binding. As well as the warden's house, the island housed around sixty members of the prison staff and their families. Until Spandau prison in Berlin was utilised for the confinement of seven Nazi war criminals, the Rock was the world's most expensive per capita prison.

One of the prison's first residents was the racketeer Alphonse Capone, America's 'Public Enemy Number One' in the Prohibition years. Capone, in fact, could be called a founder member of the island community. Indicted in Chicago for income tax evasion, he was sentenced in October 1931 to eleven years in prison and a fine of fifty thousand dollars. He began his sentence in Atlanta, but was transferred to Alcatraz in August 1933 when the first fifty-three inmates were brought to the island from Atlanta, chained hand and foot, in a special train with steel coaches and barred windows. 'Scarface' Al Capone was released – a sick man – after nearly five years on Alcatraz. He had been stabbed with a pair of scissors, and spent two years of his sentence in an isolation cell in the prison infirmary for that and other reasons. The king of vice had lost not only his crown, but his brain, too, as a result of syphilis. When reporters asked his accountant, Jake Guzik, if Capone would resume his position as boss of the Chicago underworld, Guzik replied, 'Al's as nutty as a fruit cake.'

Another sometime resident on Alcatraz was George 'Machine-Gun' Kelly, an Irish immigrant hoodlum who had kidnapped the oil tycoon Charles Urschel in Oklahoma City in 1933 and successfully ransomed him for two hundred thousand dollars, but was captured two months later. He was given a life sentence, after sending threatening letters to Urschel, the trial judge, and the head of the FBI, J. Edgar Hoover. Kelly was in Alcatraz until the early fifties, and died in 1954.

'Alcatraz gets all the rotten apples out of the barrel,' said Warden Edwin Swope when he was appointed in 1948 to succeed the retiring Warden Johnston, who had been in charge since Alcatraz had opened in 1933. The prison had been referred to as a 'hell hole' by the US Attorney-General, no less. Homosexuals among the inmates found opportunities for sexual acts by concealing themselves in the kitchen, the laundry and the shower room. Convicts committed suicide or went insane. They had been known to save or cough up sleeping pills until they had collected enough to take a fatal overdose. In 1937 a prisoner named Percival severed one of his hands with a meat cleaver and begged a fellow-convict to chop off his other hand.

The very fact that Alcatraz was designed to be the most secure federal prison for long-term convicts meant that the idea of escape became, almost from its inception, predominant in the thinking of many of its inmates. Over the years, thirty-six men made serious attempts at escape, but no one is known to have succeeded in escaping from Alcatraz, despite the fact that some of the most ingenious attempts in American penal history occurred there. In 1944, Floyd Hamilton was one of two men retaken on the island after an escape attempt involving three others. One of them was recaptured in the water and another shot dead. Hamilton, who had been the driver for Bonnie Parker and Clyde Barrow in their bank raids, hid for two days before his recapture. In 1945 one John Giles made it to the Angel Island army base on a supply boat, but was arrested as soon as he landed, by guards who had realised he was on the boat and got to the island before him. The only man definitely known to have reached the mainland through the icy waters of the bay – a distance of just over a mile – was Paul Scott, who was apprehended immediately he came ashore, half dead from hypothermia, in December 1962.

Over the years, several other would-be escapees were recaptured in the water, and five were shot dead while they were still on the island. Of the rest, one is known to have drowned and the others were presumed drowned. Doctors reckoned that a reasonably fit man could last about twenty-two minutes at most in these permanently cold and turbulent waters which rush into the Pacific Ocean, the swift currents keeping the water temperature at about seven degrees Celsius. So the odds were always against success. When the then world champion swimmer, Johnny Weismuller, considered the prospect as a publicity stunt, he decided against it.

In May 1946, the mind of a prisoner in D Block gave way, and he screamed and yelled, causing an uproar among his fellow-prisoners, who began rioting and damaging their cells. One guard was killed and others wounded in an escape bid, and the island was soon in a state of siege, which journalists quickly labelled the 'Battle of Alcatraz'. 'An inferno of gunfire between guards and rioting convicts', the *San Francisco Chronicle* reported on 3 May, 'still engulfed the Federal penitentiary on Alcatraz Island early this morning after a day and night of one of the bloodiest prison uprisings in

California history.' US Marines had landed, as well as armed San Francisco police officers and prison guard reinforcements from San Quentin, whilst Navy destroyers and Coast Guard ships patrolled the waters round the island. Windows and ceiling lights in C and D blocks were shot out, then hand-grenades and tear-gas thrown in. The buildings were shelled from ships in the bay. Mattresses and bedding were set alight, and water pipes were hit and cell floors flooded.

The armed convicts eventually had nine officers as hostages, but during the gun battle, one was shot in the back and another in the head at point-blank range, the bullet entering near his left eye and coming out near his right ear. The siege and bombardment ended on the morning of 4 May. Two prisons officers and the three leading mutineers, Coy, Hubbard and Cretzer, were dead, and one prisoner and fourteen officers wounded. Two other mutineers, Thompson and Shockley, were subsequently executed in the gas chamber at San Quentin.

One of the most famous prisoners of Alcatraz was Robert Stroud. In January 1909, when he was nineteen years old, Stroud had shot a bartender who had beaten up his (Stroud's) prostitute girlfriend. He had given himself up straight away, and was sentenced to twelve years in the penitentiary on McNeil Island, near Seattle. In 1912 he was transferred to a new maximum security prison at Leavenworth, near Kansas City. Here in 1916 he stabbed a guard to death, and was sentenced to be hanged. After desperate appeals by his mother, his sentence was commuted to life imprisonment in 1920 by the ailing President, Woodrow Wilson. It was in Leavenworth that Stroud's interest in some fledgling sparrows led to his in-depth studies of birds and their diseases. But although he became a world-famous authority on the subject, the nickname 'Bird Man of Alcatraz' is a romantic fiction.

In December 1942, Stroud left Leavenworth in handcuffs and leg-irons for Alcatraz. He was considered insane by some prison authorities, and though dangerous public enemies were allowed to associate with one another at Alcatraz, Stroud was kept in seclusion, in D Block. He was a consistent troublemaker and had been an active homosexual. He was allowed to continue his writing and studies, but not to keep birds. Warden Swope, a hardliner, later reduced even Stroud's study facilities. The US Board of Parole considered his case on several occasions, but repeatedly declared him unfit for release. In December 1951, Stroud tried to commit suicide with an overdose of pills he had stored up instead of taking them for a painful gall-bladder condition. No. 594 Stroud, occupying Cell 41 on the third tier of D Block, was, at sixty-two, the oldest man on the Rock. He had spent most of his forty-four years in prison in isolation.

Clyde Johnson, a forty-year-old bank-robber, and Aaron Burgett, a twenty-eight-year-old gangster, were among the last prisoners to make a getaway from the island, in September 1958. Johnson was quickly recaptured in the water, but it seemed that Burgett had succeeded in making his escape. More than a fortnight later, however, his ghastly remains were found floating in the bay.

In 1962, four inmates, John and Clarence Anglin, Frank Morris and a convict named West, planned to escape by removing metal grates in the walls of their cells and enlarging the holes with sharpened spoon handles so that they could get out into a utility corridor. West failed to make his hole big enough, and never got out of his cell. The other three, having fashioned dummy heads with papier mâché, and adding hair which they had taken from the barber's shop, left them in their beds on the night of 11 June, to delay discovery of their disappearance, and succeeded in getting into the corridor and crawling up a ventilation duct. They left the island on rafts made up of old raincoats, blown up with the bellows of Morris's accordion, and were never heard of again. The authorities naturally like to consider it fairly certain that all three drowned in the attempt. Romantics prefer to think that at least one of them may have made it.

On 21 March 1963, a few months after the only man known to have reached the mainland shore was recaptured, the US government, whose Attorney-General at the time was Robert Kennedy, abandoned Alcatraz Island as being too expensive to run. Its costs had been at least twice those of any other federal prison, and its buildings were deteriorating rapidly due to the salt air. It had been a federal prison for a mere twenty-nine years. One man, Alvin 'Creepy' Karpis, imprisoned for kidnapping, had been there for twenty-six of them.

Once, people gazed at Alcatraz from the shore and shuddered, perhaps, at the thought of the murderers, rapists and other hardened criminals who spent years of their lives on the Rock. Now, the island is a national park, but the prison buildings remain intact, except for the former warden's house, which was destroyed by fire in 1970 and now stands in ruins close to the lighthouse. Tourists can visit Alcatraz by boat and see for themselves what conditions were like for some of America's most notorious public enemies. In its three grim decades as one of the world's most famous prisons, Alcatraz had experienced eight murders and five suicides.

Part 3

ENEMIES OF THE STATE

INTRODUCTION

Prominent among the most infamous and controversial of the world's prisons have been those reserved not for ordinary criminals – the felons of everyday life in all countries – but for those conceived by the rulers of nations, whether kings, despots or democratic governments, as dangers to them and the security of the state – traitors and assassins, spies and subversives.

I have tried to deal strictly with established fact in this as in the other sections of the book. There are many myths about prisons abroad, perhaps calculated to comfort the British that their prisons have never been as horrific as those of wicked foreigners. But when Corfe Castle in Dorset was used as a state prison by King John, who had strengthened William the Conqueror's castle and enlarged its defences, it had an octagonal tower, called the Butavent Tower, at the western extremity, with a basement dungeon in the style of a French 'oubliette', into which neither light nor air penetrated, and the only access was by a trap-door in the floor above it. Among the King's prisoners here were twenty-two French officers, members of the Poitevin nobility, who were denied both food and water, and died of starvation. It was but one of many dark deeds enacted in Corfe's grim dungeons. A tower close by the dungeon tower was occupied by the castle's gaoler, and on the other side of the courtyard was the prison chapel. On the inner face of the enclosing wall was a gallows or 'hanging stone'.

Another prisoner here was Eleanor, the King's niece. Arthur, her brother, was the son of John's elder brother

Geoffrey, and a rival for the crown. He had been named by his uncle Richard – the 'Lionheart' – as his heir apparent. Arthur disappeared into one of John's prisons in France, and never came out alive. Eleanor spent many years at Corfe and was then moved to Bristol, where she died, having spent the greater part of her life in miserable confinement.

In 1326 the homosexual Edward II was imprisoned at Corfe before being taken to Berkeley, where he was hideously murdered by agents whose orders were to leave no marks on his body. The King's half-brother Edmund, the Earl of Kent, was convinced that Edward was still alive in the dungeons at Corfe. The castle's constable encouraged him in this delusion, and pretended to deliver messages from Kent to the captive King, but betrayed the earl to Queen Isabel and her lover, Roger Mortimer, and they ensured that Kent soon followed his brother to the grave.

Nevertheless, despite all these medieval horrors, it is certainly true that many of the hellholes of the violent century we live in, such as Somoza's prisons in Nicaragua, put in the shade the imaginary horrors of such as the old Rasphouse in Amsterdam, where it was popularly rumoured that prisoners were thrown into a flooded underground cell which contained a water pump, and that they were instantly faced with the choice between nonstop pumping or being drowned.

Some victims of national security operations, such as Dreyfus and Mandela, have already been encountered, but this part deals mainly with prisons which have been established specifically for such prisoners. If some of the prisons included here were not built for enemies of the state in the strict political sense, they were at least for what the Americans reasonably call public enemies. The exception to the rule in this section is the Black Hole of Calcutta, but that infamous dungeon would be unique

in any category of prison literature, and had to be
included somewhere.

THE TOWER OF LONDON

The British royal fortress which began with the central keep, built by William the Conqueror and known (after Henry III had its exterior walls whitewashed) as the White Tower, was gradually extended over the centuries, and each new building had its dungeon – the Lanthorn Tower; the Wakefield Tower; the Salt Tower; the Beauchamp Tower; the Byward Tower and the Bell Tower; the Well and Cradle Towers; the Bloody Tower; and so on. By the Tudor period, the Tower was more important as a state prison than as a royal palace, and as such it has a melancholy history as

> London's lasting shame,
> With many a foul and midnight murder fed.

Women feature as prominently as men among the more famous unfortunates for whom fate decreed incarceration, and sometimes death, in the dungeons of one of Europe's strongest fortresses. Among the earliest intimations of the sinister future the Tower was to have as a place of imprisonment had been the confinement, 'loaded with irons', of William le Marish and his accomplices in a plot to assassinate Henry III in 1238.

The first prisoner of the Tower whom we know of, however, was Ranulf Flambard, Bishop of Durham and chaplain to the late and unlamented William Rufus. He was arrested by order of Henry I in August 1100, less than a fortnight after the new King's accession. He did not languish too long in the Tower, making a successful escape by means of a rope at Candlemas in the following year. But when the Welsh prince Gruffyd, son of

Llewelyn the Great, attempted a similar escape from the White Tower in 1244, the rope which he had made from his sheets broke, and he plunged head-first to his death.

Scottish rulers succeeded Welsh ones as unwilling residents of the Tower. The former king, John Balliol, was kept prisoner for more than two years, probably in the Salt Tower, before being released at the request of Pope Boniface VIII, and King David II was detained and held to ransom after the battle at Neville's Cross in 1346. Among other unwilling royal guests of the English were James I of Scotland and King John of France; but it was a King of England, the feeble Henry VI, whose fate provided the most ominous sign of things to come, when he was murdered in 1471 – according to tradition, in the Wakefield Tower, whilst he was at prayer.

Six hundred Jews were imprisoned in a sub-crypt of the White Tower by Edward I in 1278, accused – no doubt falsely – of clipping coins, and nearly half of them were taken out and hanged in the following year. Of the rest, those who did not die in the Tower from starvation or other ill-treatment were banished.

The Tower was seized by rebels during the Peasants' Revolt of 1381. Four hundred armed men entered the fortress, and dragged out Archbishop Sudbury, Sir Robert Hales and John Leggs (the man who had been responsible for the hated poll tax), and executed them there and then. Simon of Sudbury was decapitated on a log of wood on Tower Hill, his executioner taking eight strokes to hack off his head, which was then paraded round the streets of London on a pike, with his bishop's mitre nailed to the skull.

It was during Edward I's reign that the water-gate was constructed beneath St Thomas's Tower to allow access to the fortress's inner ward from the Thames. This entrance was to become known in the annals of infamy as Traitor's Gate, and the most famous of the many prisoners who passed through it was the Princess

Elizabeth, committed to the Tower by her sister Mary for alleged treason. 'Here landeth the truest subject being a prisoner,' she protested as she stepped from the barge, in heavy rain, 'that ever landed at these stairs.' She spent over two months in a chamber in the Bell Tower before her release to more lenient captivity.

The most notorious part of the fortress is undoubtedly the so-called Bloody Tower, once known as the Garden Tower, where the sons of Edward IV – the twelve-year-old Edward V and his younger brother Richard, Duke of York – were murdered, almost certainly (despite several recent attempts to clear him of the crime) by order of their uncle Richard, Duke of Gloucester. Their deaths, perhaps by suffocation, probably happened in the autumn of 1483, for until the summer they had been seen 'shooting and playing in the garden of the Tower by sundry times', according to one account, but were then, according to another, 'seen more rarely behind the bars and windows, till at length they ceased to appear altogether'.

Their uncle George, Duke of Clarence, had already come to grief in the same tower, reputedly in a butt of Malmsey wine. Shakespeare represents him telling Brackenbury, the Constable of the Tower, of his nightmarish premonitions:

> Lord, Lord! methought, what pain it was to drown!
> What dreadful noise of water in mine ears!
> What ugly sights of death within mine eyes!
> Methought I saw a thousand fearful wrecks;
> Ten thousand men that fishes gnaw'd upon;
> Wedges of gold, great anchors, heaps of pearl,
> Inestimable stones, unvalued jewels
> All scatter'd in the bottom of the sea:
> Some lay in dead men's skulls; and, in those holes
> Where eyes did once inhabit, there were crept,
> As 'twere in scorn of eyes, reflecting gems,
> Which woo'd the slimy bottom of the deep,
> And mock'd the dead bones that lay scatter'd by.

A damp, gloomy vault of the Bell Tower, a 'close, filthy prison . . . among mice and rats', was where Sir Thomas More was confined in 1534, deprived at length of books, pen and ink, but continuing to write, using a piece of coal, until he was taken out and beheaded on Tower Hill. He wrote his *Dialogue of Comfort* during his time in the Tower. More refused for fifteen months to be pressurised by the King, Thomas Cromwell, or Alice, his wife, into recognising Henry VIII as the Pope's superior in England and thus gaining his freedom. Lady Alice thought him the 'foolishest wise man in the kingdom', but More said, 'Is this house not as nigh heaven as mine own?' Most would have thought it more nigh the other place.

John Fisher, Bishop of Rochester, was here at the same time as More, and for the same reason. He was in his eightieth year, and was kept in a cold, damp dungeon in winter, inadequately fed and without sufficient clothing. The old man pleaded with Thomas Cromwell for some easing of the conditions in which he was held, but to no avail, and when he was brought to the scaffold, he was so weak that he could not walk, and had to be carried.

Anne Boleyn was not long in following More and Fisher to the executioner's block, but she was beheaded privately on the green beside the White Tower, to avoid the embarrassment of a public execution. An executioner from Calais was brought over specially to do the job. The ominous precedent for executions within the Tower precincts had been set by Richard of Gloucester in his notorious *coup d'état*, when he swore that he would not dine until he had seen the severed head of William, Lord Hastings, whom he accused of treason. Hastings had promptly been taken out and beheaded on a block of wood waiting to be used in building repairs. Although some of those put to death in the Tower are recognised as cases of execution, the line between execution and murder is a thin one, and the killing of Lord Hastings, called an execution simply because it was ordered in public rather than committed in secret, was characteristic of the dark deeds that distinguish the Tower of London as a state prison where bloody murder was done on numerous occasions.

Catherine Howard and Lady Jane Grey soon joined the small number, mostly women, known to have been beheaded within the Tower precincts. The sixteen-year-old Jane saw the decapitated corpse of her husband, Lord Guildford Dudley, being brought back from Tower Hill for burial, before she was led to her own appalling end, an innocent victim of political scheming by her relatives. She was not executed in public on Tower Hill, for fear of provoking another switch in the fickle loyalties of the populace. A handkerchief was tied over her eyes as she stood on the fresh straw scattered round the block to soak up her blood. Asking the executioner to dispatch her quickly, she reached out with her hands, saying, 'What shall I do? Where is it?' They guided her to the block and the deed was done. Her head and body were buried in the chapel of St Peter-ad-Vincula, and when the coffin was opened, many years later, the remains crumbled to dust immediately on exposure to the air.

The nine-day-Queen's young sister Katherine – the so-called 'Lady of Lamentations' – also spent some time in the Tower, and gave birth to her two children there, before being removed, when the plague was raging in London, to be confined in other places, and enforceably separated from her husband, until her death at the age of thirty.

The last victim of the headsman's axe within the Tower itself was the Earl of Essex in 1601, although many others went out from here to their executions elsewhere – noblemen usually just outside the walls, on Tower Hill, and commoners at Tyburn.

Sir Walter Raleigh was as familiar with the doleful prison as were its keepers. He was committed to it first in 1592 by Queen Elizabeth for allegedly seducing one of her ladies-in-waiting, Elizabeth Throgmorton. He was in the Tower only briefly on this occasion – three or four months. But he returned to it in 1603 on the orders of James I. Raleigh had been convicted of treason for plotting to bring Lady Arabella Stuart – a descendant of Henry VII – to the English throne, and he was sentenced to death, but reprieved. He spent nearly fourteen years in the Bloody Tower. He was permitted to live on an upper floor with his wife and son, and to turn a hen-house into a laboratory where he could study chemistry. He also wrote his *History of the World* whilst in prison. The King released Raleigh in 1617 to lead an expedition to South America in search of gold, but the quest was a failure, and on its return the unfortunate Raleigh – sixty-five years old and already a dying man – was again committed to the Tower, and this time executed without trial, the merciless King claiming the earlier overturned sentence as his justification.

Arabella Stuart, meanwhile, the King's cousin, had died 'distracted' – a euphemism for insane – in the Tower, after being imprisoned for secretly marrying William Seymour, another claimant to the throne.

Archbishop Laud was another prisoner of the Bloody Tower before his execution on Tower Hill; and the savage Baron Wem, Judge Jeffreys, the most hated man of his time in England, died here in 1689, tormented by disease, a 'pitiable spectacle' as Macaulay tells us, emaciated and sodden with brandy, but defending his appalling actions to the end.

The Tower's dungeons had become the condemned cells of many illustrious captives sentenced to execution, and many prisoners with time at their disposal scratched inscriptions on the bare stone walls of their prisons. Some of them are simply names, like the one word

'Jane', supposed to have been carved on a wall of the Beauchamp Tower by the doomed Guildford Dudley; and that of 'Edmonde Poole', who spent seven years in the Tower for his involvement in a conspiracy against Elizabeth I, and died here in 1570. 'John Talbot, 1462' is one of the oldest inscriptions on these recording stones. Some are devotional aids scratched by Catholic recusants. The 'IHS' monogram was carved more than once by Jesuit prisoners. Some are much more elaborate carvings, with ornamented mottoes in Latin, or personal records in English, like that of the Irish rebel Thomas Miagh in the Beauchamp Tower:

> Thomas Miagh which lieth here alon
> That fayne would from hens be gon
> By torture straunge mi trouth was tryed
> Yet of my libertie denied
> 1581 Thomas Myagh

Miagh was detained in the Tower for two and a half years, and tortured with 'Skevington's Irons' and on the rack, but admitted nothing and was eventually released for lack of evidence.

The irons, named after their inventor, held the prisoner in a vice-like grip in a hideously painful half-standing, half-stooping position. The rack, a machine which could reputedly make its victims a foot longer than their natural length by stretching their arms and legs in opposite directions by means of ropes wound on rollers, is believed to have been used in the basement of the Wakefield Tower. Another torture peculiar to the Tower was to be locked in a dungeon which was below the water line at high tide, and with the rising river water came rats, so that a prisoner could not sleep for fear of being either drowned or eaten alive.

Torture was forbidden under English law, but the royal prerogative was considered to be above the law by those who employed it. As Macaulay wrote: 'Those rulers who had occasionally resorted to it had, as far as was possible, used it in secret, had never pretended that they had acted in conformity with either statute law or common law, and had excused themselves by saying that the extraordinary peril to which the state was exposed had forced them to take on themselves the responsibility of employing extraordinary means of defence.' Many prisoners of the Crown were racked or otherwise tortured with this lame excuse during the fifteenth and succeeding two centuries; none more so than the victims of the most shameful episode in the Tower's grim history – the period of religious persecution under the Tudors and Stuarts.

The Protestants tortured in the Tower included Mistress Anne Askew, who suffered on the rack in 1546 before being taken to Smithfield to be burned at the stake for denying the doctrine of transubstantiation: '. . . because I lay still and did not cry,' she alleged, 'my Lord Chancellor and Master Rich took pains to rack me with their own hands . . .'. Anne Askew 'abode their tyranny till her bones and joints were almost plucked asunder', and she had to be carried in a chair to Smithfield because she 'could not walk on her feet by means of her great torments'. Under Bloody Mary, the crippling of Cuthbert Simpson is depicted in a contemporary engraving, the first to show the rack in use. Before going on the rack, Simpson had his forefingers bound together and a small arrow was put between them and pulled through 'so fast that blood flowed and the arrow broke. Then they racked me twice.' Simpson was also put into 'Skevington's gyves' for three hours.

Elizabeth I made it an act of high treason to maintain the Pope's authority in England, or to be a Jesuit, seminary priest, 'and such other like disobedient persons'. The Jesuit Edmund Campion, during his first visit to the Tower, was put in a cell called 'Little Ease' – a tiny room so constructed that one could neither stand up, sit, nor lie down at full length. Prisoners condemned to it had to adopt a cramped squatting posture which grew the more intolerable the longer they were left there. Campion endured this, and was released, but was arrested again and severely racked, before being taken to be hanged, disembowelled and quartered at Tyburn in 1581.

The Jesuit priest John Gerard was held here for three years in 'Good Queen Bess's' reign, accused of plotting against the state. He had 'been examined time and time again, and they had not produced a scrap of writing or a single trustworthy witness to show that I had taken part in any activities against the government.' But when he refused to give information about others whom he knew to be equally innocent, '. . . they produced a warrant for putting me to torture. They had it ready by them and handed it to me to read. (In this prison a special warrant is required for torture.)' The guards took him to the torture room in a solemn procession. It was mid-April 1597. 'The chamber was underground and dark, particularly near the entrance. It was a vast place and every device and instrument of human torture was there.'

They asked Father Gerard again if he would confess, and when he said he could not, they allowed him to pray for a moment. Then,

they took me to a big upright pillar, one of the wooden posts which held the roof of this huge underground chamber. Driven in to the top of it were iron staples for supporting heavy weights. Then they put my wrists into iron gauntlets and ordered me to climb two or three wicker steps. My arms were then lifted up and an iron bar was passed through the rings of one gauntlet, then through the staple and rings of the second gauntlet. This done, they fastened the bar with a pin to prevent it slipping, and then, removing the wicker steps one by one from under my feet, they left me hanging by my hands and arms fastened above my head. The tips of my toes, however, still touched the ground, and they had to dig away the earth from under them. They had hung me from the highest staple in the pillar and could not raise me any higher, without driving in another staple.

The torturers again pressed Gerard to confess, but he refused, and was overcome by pain.

> It was worst in my chest and belly, my hands and arms. All the blood in my body seemed to rush up into my arms and hands and I thought that blood was oozing out from the ends of my fingers and the pores of my skin. But it was only a sensation caused by my flesh swelling above the irons holding them. The pain was so intense that I thought I could not possibly endure it . . .

After being taken to the torture chamber twice more, Father Gerard managed to escape; unlike Nicholas Owen, the Jesuit who became well known for the ingenuity of the hiding places he constructed for his persecuted Catholic brethren in houses all over the country. Owen died under torture in the Tower on 2 March 1606.

When the famous wit and Member of Parliament John Wilkes was committed by the government of Lord Bute to the Tower in April 1763 for seditious libel, after publishing his famous attack on the King's speech, he is said to have asked for a room, if it were possible to find one, where no Scotchman had been imprisoned, because he was afraid of catching the itch! Wilkes spent only a few days here, and the general warrant by which he was imprisoned, without a specific charge being made against him, was turned to his advantage, for he was able to liken its vague legality to the French *lettre de cachet*; and indeed, when his friend Earl Temple, the richest commoner in England, was refused access to Wilkes, he was moved to reflect that 'I thought this was the Tower, but I find it is the Bastille.'

Lord George Gordon was imprisoned in the Tower in

1780 for eight months, charged with high treason after instigating the Gordon Riots (see Newgate). But he was eventually acquitted on grounds of insanity, aged thirty.

Sir Roger Casement was held briefly in the Tower for treason during the First World War, and it was alleged by his cousin, Gertrude Bannister, that the dark cell, where he was guarded night and day by two soldiers, was verminous, and that Casement had bites on his head, neck and arms. Rumours circulated that Casement was to be shot at once, and Casement himself believed this was to be his fate. In fact, he was removed to Brixton prison, where he remained during his trial, eventually to be hanged at Pentonville.

It is sometimes said that the seven known to have been beheaded in the Tower were the only people *executed* within the Tower precincts. This is certainly not the case. In 1743, for instance, three deserters from a Scottish regiment were shot by firing squad on Tower Green. And during the two world wars, a number of spies were shot by firing squad here. Eleven were shot during the 1914–18 war in a rifle range adjoining the Martin Tower. And in the 1939–45 war, a German spy named Josef Jakobs, who parachuted into the country wearing a pinstriped suit and spats, and carrying a bowler hat, was shot on 15 August 1941. During the same year, Rudolf Hess, Hitler's former deputy, was held briefly in the Tower, one of the old fortress's last prisoners.

The Bastille was begun by Charles V of France around 1370, and was built by forced labour, being completed in 1382. Paris's new citadel was officially known then as the castle of St Antoine, but the Parisians called the fortress 'la Bastille', which meant only 'castle with towers', and it was hardly unique in that respect. The towers were eight stone bastions. The castle was surrounded by a wall sixty feet high, and by a wide ditch, crossed by a drawbridge. The name St Antoine is still in use for one of the streets leading to its original site on the west side of the present Place de la Bastille.

In due course, Cardinal Richelieu converted the 'Bastille' into a state prison, used for political prisoners and persons of rank, and people were committed to it by *lettres de cachet* – documents of royal authority which permitted the detention of prisoners for long periods without trial. The prison came to be hated by the populace of Paris as a symbol of tyranny and injustice, and its fall in the French Revolution was not the first time it was attacked. It had been forced to surrender to the Catholic League under the Duke of Guise on 14 May 1588, following the 'Day of the Barricades' during the French wars of religion.

Many prisoners spent large parts of their lives in the Bastille. François de Bassompierre, the soldier and diplomat, was sent there by Richelieu in 1631 for his support of Marie de' Medici, and remained there for twelve years, until Richelieu's death, writing his memoirs in prison.

Henri de Latude made daring escapes from the

Bastille three times during his sentence of twenty-eight years, from 1749, for inventing a plot to poison Madame de Pompadour, in order to win her favour by revealing it. He was released in 1777 only on condition that he returned to his native Languedoc, and when he was found to be still in Paris, he was sent back to the dread prison for a few more years.

Of shorter duration was the imprisonment in 1679 of Catherine Deshayes, Madame Monvoisin, a 'witch' known as 'La Voisin', who went to the Bastille when it was found that she had been dealing in poisons with high-society ladies who wanted to be rid of their husbands. She had poisoned her own husband, too, and was alleged to have performed a great many abortions and to have killed unwanted babies. In the following year, La Voisin was burned at the stake.

The place must have been a kind of hell for the Bastille's most famous prisoner – a man with no name – in spite of the material comforts provided for him. He arrived in September 1698, in the company of the newly appointed governor, Monsieur de St Mars, who had had the prisoner in his charge during two previous governor-ships, at the fortress of Pignerol, near Turin, and on the island of Sainte-Marguerite, off Cannes. The prisoner travelled to the Bastille from the south in a litter, with a mask of black velvet over his face, lest anyone should recognise him during the journey, and his identity remains a mystery to this day. He became known, erroneously, as the 'Man in the Iron Mask'.

This prisoner of the 'Sun King', Louis XIV, told a doctor in the Bastille that he was about sixty years old, and a prisoner named de Renneville, who saw the masked man there, claimed to have been told by a turnkey that the mystery man had been a prisoner for thirty-one years. He was said to have white hair, and was treated with great deference by his captors. He was a Catholic, for he attended mass, always masked, in the

Bastille chapel. His identity was a state secret, and immense security measures always surrounded him. He was said to live under the threat of instant death if he should ever attempt to identify himself or show his face to anyone. He was known to his fellow prisoners simply as 'La Tour', because of the location of his room or cell.

On 19 March 1703, the mysterious prisoner apparently died in the Bastille, and on the following day, his coffin – into which chemicals were put to hasten decomposition of the corpse – was carried along the road from the prison to St Paul's churchyard for burial, under the supervision of the prison surgeon and the deputy-governor. The deceased was identified in the church register only as one 'Marchioly, aged 45 or thereabouts'. It is said that even the two senior Bastille officials did not know his true identity.

Back in the Bastille, everything in the room the prisoner had occupied – table and chairs, clothes and blankets – was burnt. The walls were scraped and whitewashed, and the floor tiles taken up and replaced. There was to be no trace left of this prisoner for anyone to find. It was as if he had never existed. The last person believed to know the truth about the masked man was the Sun King's great-grandson, Louis XV. The secret died with him.

There have been many theories about the identity of the so-called Man in the Iron Mask. Voltaire believed he was an illegitimate son of Anne of Austria and Cardinal Mazarin and, as the elder brother of Louis, rightful heir to the throne. Dumas believed he was a twin brother of Louis. Another theory is that the prisoner was Eustache d'Auger de Cavoye, whose father had been an officer under Richelieu. D'Auger, this speculation goes, must have stumbled upon a state secret – that his father had, as a service to his country, fathered Louis XIV on Anne of Austria in order to secure the succession, which Louis XIII had been physically incapable of doing. But as

Eustache was the spitting image of his half-brother, the reasoning goes, the very sight of him would have given the game away, so he had to be hidden, as well as silenced.

The trouble with all these theories is that Louis XIV was a ruthless monarch, capable of any cruelty, and he would hardly have hesitated, through family sentiment, to order the secret assassination of the one man who could reveal that he, Louis, was not the rightful occupant of the French throne. Louis sent the Duc de La Force to the Bastille in 1689 for being a Protestant. Nearly sixty years old, the prisoner spent four years there and suffered from dropsy through lack of exercise. Moreover, the Sun King had no qualms about sending women of class to his awful state dungeons. He committed Jeanne-Marie Bouvier de La Motte, Madame Guyen du Chesnoy, to the Bastille in 1695 for eight years. A pious widow, she had caused controversy with her unorthodox beliefs and mysticism. She was in the Bastille when the Man in the Iron Mask arrived.

Some historians believe the masked prisoner to have been the Italian diplomat, Count Mattioli, foreign secretary to the Duke of Mantua. But his arrest and imprisonment were no secret, and there was no known reason for going to such extraordinary lengths to hide his identity. And even if there were, the use of the name 'Marchioly' at his burial would hardly have been intelligent. Besides, all the evidence suggests that Mattioli died on Sainte-Marguerite in 1694, and never went to the Bastille, whose masked prisoner remains one of history's best-kept secrets.

Voltaire himself was twice a prisoner of the Bastille when a young man. In 1717, in his early twenties, Jean François Marie Arouet, then intent on epic poetry rather than satirical prose, was committed by *lettre de cachet* to the fortress for writing a scurrilous lampoon on the regent, Philippe, Duc d'Orleans. Voltaire described the Bastille as a

> Palace of vengeance, dark and bodeful pile,
> Where languish, side by side, the pure, the vile.

Voltaire languished there himself for eighteen months, and told the duke after his release that in future he would be gratified by the Regent's provision of his board, but not his lodging. He did see the inside of the Bastille again, nevertheless. He was committed there a second time through the influence of the Chevalier de Rohan-Chabot, who deliberately insulted the young poet at the Paris Opera, and also had him beaten up by a gang of armed thugs. Voltaire was released after a few days this time, but only on condition that he left France.

Count Alessandro di Cagliostro and Cardinal Rohan-Guemenee ended up in the Bastille in 1785 after the famous affair in which they were involved with the Comtesse de La Motte, who was branded and imprisoned for an elaborate con-trick to cheat a jeweller out of a diamond necklace he understood to be for the Queen.

John Howard's *State of the Prisons* included a French description of the Bastille as it existed just a few years before the Revolution:

> The dungeons at the bottom of the towers exhale the most offensive scents, and are the receptacles of toads, rats, and other kinds of vermin. In the corner of each is a camp-bed, made of planks laid on iron bars that are fixed on the walls, and the prisoners are allowed some straw to lay on the beds. These dens are dark, having no windows, but openings into the ditch: they have double doors, the inner ones plated with iron, with large bolts and locks.
>
> Of the five classes of chambers, the most horrid next to the dungeons are those in which are cages of iron. There are three of them. They are formed of beams with strong plates of iron, and are each eight feet by six.
>
> The *calottes*, or chambers at the top of the towers, are

somewhat more tolerable. They are formed of eight arcades of freestone. Here one cannot walk but in the middle of the room. There is hardly sufficient space for a bed from one arcade to another. The windows, being in walls ten feet thick, and having iron gates within and without, admit but little light. In these rooms the heat is excessive in summer, and the cold in winter. They have stoves.

Almost all the other rooms (of the towers) are octagons, about twenty feet in diameter, and from fourteen to fifteen high. They are very cold and damp. Each is furnished with a bed of green serge, etc. All the chambers are numbered. The prisoners are called by the name of their tower joined to the number of their room.

Charles Dickens represented Dr Manette, in *A Tale of Two Cities*, as having spent nearly eighteen years in the Bastille before being freed, a demented and white-haired old man, still answering, when asked his name, 'One Hundred and Five, North Tower'. Dickens painted the same dolorous image of the solitary continental dungeon as Alexandre Dumas was soon to do in *The Count of Monte Cristo*, in contrast to the common English dungeon which tended rather to be a crowded and fetid cell. The Comte de Lauzun, confined in a dark dungeon at Pignerol for nine years, is said to have come close to death from grief when a keeper trod on his only companion, a spider. But life was not necessarily all that bad for most of the Bastille's prisoners, despite the lurid accounts published by the journalist Simon Linguet, who was in the Bastille in 1780–2, of the sufferings of those consigned to it. The wealthier ones could live in relative luxury in private apartments and dine in the company of family and friends, attended by their servants. The Bastille's place in this present volume is due rather to its exaggerated notoriety than to its inhuman conditions.

Among the Bastille's last prisoners was the Marquis de Sade, who had been condemned to death in Aix for his cruelty and unnatural practices, but lived to go to the Bastille and write some of his notorious books there. Early in July 1789, de Sade was removed from the Bastille and taken to the asylum for the insane at Charenton, where he died a quarter of a century later. It would have been a nice irony if, left in the prison for another ten or eleven days, one of the pathetic inmates released by the Paris mob had been this aristocratic pervert.

The storming of the Bastille, on 14 July 1789, is seen in retrospect as the first great symbolic act of the French Revolution. A Paris mob – consisting mostly of local tradesmen and workers, though described by Tom Paine as 'a vast mixed multitude of all ages, and of all degrees, armed with all sorts of weapons' – marched on this monument to royal despotism, which was also a government arsenal, and demanded that the governor, de Launay, hand over the arms, consisting of cartridges and two hundred and fifty barrels of gunpowder, to them. He refused, so the crowd forced an entry to the inner courtyard, where panicking soldiers opened fire on them. Aided by some of the guards, who switched their allegiance to the populace, the crowd attacked. Nearly a hundred of them were killed, and seventy-three wounded, as well as several defenders, before the governor surrendered.

The mob discovered in this labyrinth of towers, bastions and drawbridges – this great symbol of oppression – a mere seven prisoners, who were released after being carried through the streets in triumph. They comprised two lunatics, four forgers and one nobleman (the old and emaciated Comte de Lorge, who had been there, almost forgotten, for thirty years).

The rioters dragged the governor to the Place de Grève, where they hacked him to pieces and paraded his head on a pike. De Launay's was the first severed head from which the young Marie Grozholtz, soon to be famous as Madame Tussaud, took a death mask.

Before the month was out, workmen – some of whom had previously been unemployed – were busy demolishing the old fortress in its entirety. Not a stone was to be left standing. The demolition gangs stood on the walls and smashed them from beneath their feet, much as exuberant Germans demolished the Berlin Wall in more recent times. Parisians danced on the ruins. The place was subsequently converted into a woodyard, and the Bastille's site is today marked out by lines of white stones in the Place de la Bastille and Boulevard Henri IV. Much of the Bastille's stone was used to build the Pont de la Concorde over the Seine.

When Edmund Burke denounced the revolution in his *Reflections on the Revolution in France*, and lamented that 'The age of chivalry is gone!', Thomas Paine retorted, in *The Rights of Man*:

> Through the whole of Mr Burke's book I do not observe that the Bastille is mentioned more than once, and that with a kind of implication as if he were sorry it was pulled down, and wished it were built up again. 'We have rebuilt Newgate,' says he, 'and tenanted the mansion; and we have prisons almost as strong as the Bastille for those who dare to libel the Queens of France.' ... Not one glance of compassion, not one commiserating reflection that I can find throughout his book, has he bestowed on those who lingered out the most wretched of lives, a life without hope in the most miserable of prisons.

No prison anywhere in the world, probably, has aroused stronger emotions than the Bastille of Paris, and its destruction, regardless of the merits of the Revolution as a whole, was undoubtedly a blessing. The fall of the Bastille was greeted with joy far beyond the borders of France. The event was the talk of Europe. In England, Charles James Fox called it the greatest and best event in history, and in Russia, people danced in the streets of St Petersburg. 'The cry of freedom rings in my ears,' wrote Count Stroganov, who was present when the Bastille fell, 'and the best day of my life will be when I see Russia regenerated by such a revolution.'

3

THE PRISONS OF PARIS IN THE REVOLUTION

The first act of the revolutionary mob in Paris may have been to storm and destroy the hated Bastille, but the cry of 'Liberté! Egalité! Fraternité!' did not fool anyone into thinking that there would be no further need for gaols. The Temple – the keep or donjon of the former fortress of the knights Templars – was quickly utilised as a state prison, and the city's main criminal prison was even older than the destroyed Bastille.

The chief criminal prison in the whole of France before the Revolution was the fortress of Grand Châtelet. It was originally built in the ninth century, and stood at the centre of Paris near the Hôtel de Ville and the cathedral of Notre Dame. It always had a terrible reputation. The ground-floor cells were for poor prisoners who slept on straw on the stone floors. Above were rooms for those who could afford to pay for more tolerable conditions. The fortress had dungeons known as 'The Ditch', 'Barbary' and 'End of Ease', and the Oubliette, a deep hole into which prisoners were lowered with ropes through a trap-door, and from which they might never emerge alive. Among the prisoners held in the Grand Châtelet was the unruly poet François Villon, who was twice sentenced to death in the fifteenth century, but reprieved both times. He swore that conditions in the prison were worse than hell. The Petit Châtelet was a later extension. Its dungeons were so badly ventilated that some prisoners died within days of being shut up in them.

The Conciergerie, nearby on the Île de la Cité, and dating back to the eleventh century, was originally built to house Philippe-le-Bel's palace guards and his concierge (then master of the royal household – not merely a caretaker or doorkeeper, as the word implies now). Part of it became a prison in 1391 as an annex of the Châtelet, but its importance increased as time went on. Before the present Quai de l'Horloge was built along its river front, its cells were frequently flooded. Its prisoners before the Revolution included François Ravaillac, the assassin of Henri IV, and Marie Madeleine, Marquise de Brinvilliers. Ravaillac, a fanatical Catholic schoolmaster, was taken from here in 1610 to his execution, the *amende honorable*, which was intended as an exemplar of terror for the populace. Bound to the scaffold, Ravaillac first had the hand with which he had stabbed the King burnt off. Then lumps of flesh were torn from various parts of his body with red-hot pincers, and scalding pitch and brimstone were poured into his wounds, while the wretched, shrieking Ravaillac was exhorted to reveal the names of his accomplices. Finally, his limbs were tied to four horses which were driven to tear him apart, but could only do so when the executioner had severed the sinews with a knife.

The Marquise de Brinvilliers was a multiple murderess, who poisoned several members of her family. She learned the means from her lover, Jean Baptiste de Gaudin, Seigneur de Sainte-Croix, who had picked up the method from a prisoner in the Bastille, where he had been committed by the marquise's father, one of her subsequent victims. But her attempt to poison her husband the marquis failed, and her crimes were discovered. She was executed in 1676.

After the fall of the Bastille, the Châtelet and Conciergerie were supplemented by commandeering other establishments for use as temporary prisons. They included the Luxembourg Palace, the Salpêtrière hospital for insane women and prostitutes, the Bicêtre hospital, La Force, the debtors' prison, and the Abbaye, a former Carmelite convent on the Quai de la Mêgisserie. The latter was below the level of the Seine, and prisoners were drowned in it when the river was in flood.

There were three thousand counter-revolutionaries and ordinary criminals in these prisons in 1792 when advancing Prussian and Austrian armies threatened Paris with invasion. Thousands of volunteers were prepared to leave Paris at Danton's call, to join the battle to defend the city, but Marat warned them that if they deserted their families before dealing with the dangerous traitors in their midst, a mass escape might occur, with terrible consequences. 'We go to fight the enemy,' Marat said, 'but we will not leave robbers behind us, to butcher our wives and children.' This incitement resulted in the September Massacres. Armed and undisciplined gangs broke into the prisons and slaughtered around 1,500 people, half the prison population. Terrified prisoners trembled in the shadows as mobs with clothes and weapons soaked in blood smashed their cell doors and burst in to drag them out and dispense immediate 'justice' to those found guilty in travesties of trials by kangaroo courts. At three o'clock in the morning, one witness recorded in the Abbaye:

> They were breaking in one of the prison doors. We at first thought they were coming to kill us in our room; but heard, by voices on the staircase, that it was a room where some prisoners had barricaded themselves. They were all butchered there, as we shortly gathered.

Some victims in the prison were merely thieves and forgers convicted of being royalist plotters. Two hundred priests were slaughtered. The frenzied sansculottes murdered screaming prisoners and insane patients, raping women and obscenely mutilating them. Marie, Princess de Lamballe, the Queen's favourite, held in La Force, was decapitated, and her head was stuck on a pike and set up outside the window of Marie Antoinette's apartment in the Temple. One woman had her breasts cut off and was then nailed to the ground by her feet with a fire between her parted legs. Nearly four hundred prisoners in the Conciergerie were butchered. Their bloody corpses were piled up in the Cour du Mai to be carted away for mass burial.

The September Massacres were the beginning of the Terror in France, and the Conciergerie, in particular, became the most infamous of the Paris prisons during that bloody period. Over four thousand citizens of Paris were held in it, of whom more than half, after their napes had been shaved and their hands tied behind their backs, went on tumbrils to the guillotine. Marie Antoinette was held prisoner there from August 2 until October 16 1793, carnations being brought for her cell every day by the concierge, before she went to her own end, following her husband, Louis Capet, hitherto King Louis XVI of France, who had been held in the Temple prior to his trial and execution, along with his son Charles Louis, the nine-year-old Dauphin, whose fate is unknown.

Each day terrified prisoners – aristocratic men and women, royalists, counter-revolutionaries and clergymen – listened to the roll-call of the condemned, hoping against hope that their names were not on it. If their names *were* called out, they had but a short time to part from their loved ones and prepare themselves for death. They came out of the prisons in a seemingly endless procession – Princess Elizabeth, the King's thirty-year-old sister; Madame du Barry, Louis XV's mistress; Charlotte Corday, the murderer of Marat; Madame Roland (wife of the former minister of the interior), who had been held in the Abbaye and at Sainte-Pelagie; the Duke and Duchess of Noailles; the Vicomte de Beauharnais; the former minister Malesherbes, seventy-three years old, along with his daughter and son-in-law.

As the prisons overflowed with suspects, the guillotine could scarcely cope with the number of its clients. From the Luxembourg and the Châtelet, the Temple and La Force, the Salpêtrière, the Bicêtre and the Abbaye the victims were transferred to the Conciergerie, which served as a transit camp en route to the rendezvous with Madame Guillotine in the Place de la Revolution. But at last the tide turned against the executioners, and Desmoulins and Danton, the chief creators of the Terror, were arrested and taken to the Luxembourg, but not to linger there, for after three days they went to their deaths, Danton predicting that Robespierre would follow hot on his heels. And at last the cells of the Conciergerie held, only briefly, the appalling *citoyens* Saint-Just and Robespierre, the latter having failed in a messy attempt to shoot himself.

After the Revolution, the Luxembourg Palace and the Salpêtrière and Bicêtre reverted to their original purpose. Le Châtelet was demolished in 1802 and the Temple six years later. The Conciergerie remained a prison until 1914. Parts of it are now open to the public. Marie Antoinette's cell has been re-created at one end of the Galerie des Prisonniers. The actual cell was on the site of the altar of the Chapelle des Girondins. An aisle in the Gothic hall known as the Salle des Gens d'Armes is calles 'Rue de Paris'. It was the route taken regularly during the Terror by the man known as Monsieur de Paris – the executioner Sanson. One of his guillotine blades is on display.

4

PRISONS OF THE INQUISITION

> The blackness of eternal night encompassed me. I struggled
> for breath. The intensity of the darkness seemed to oppress
> and stifle me. The atmosphere was intolerably close. I still
> lay quietly, and made effort to exercise my reason . . .
>
> And now . . . there came thronging upon my recollection
> a thousand vague rumours of the horrors of Toledo. Of the
> dungeons there had been strange things narrated – fables I
> had always deemed them – but yet strange, and too ghastly
> to repeat, save in a whisper.

The narrator is the nameless victim of Edgar Allan Poe's
classic tale, *The Pit and the Pendulum*, lying in the
Inquisition's stone vault and awaiting his doom. But
Poe's fiction was not so far in excess of fact as to be called
sheer fantasy. The fear of torture and of death was a
constant factor in the waking hours of those prisoners of
the Holy Office accused of heresy from about the middle
of the thirteenth century. Perpetual imprisonment was
the common punishment for those heretics who
repented, in accordance with a Bull of Gregory IX in
1231. But the dreadful possibility of torture must always
have been in the minds of those condemned, for the
whole purpose of the Inquisition was to stem the tide of
heresy and bring the guilty back to orthodoxy, by fair
means or foul. Pope Clement V acknowledged in 1306
that prisoners were 'habitually constrained to confession by the harshness of the prison, the lack of beds, and
the deficiency of food, as well as by torture'.

Joan of Arc, held for months and interrogated in a
cold stone dungeon in the castle at Rouen in 1431, was

taken at last to a tower where Pierre Cauchon, Bishop of Beauvais, awaited her with other inquisitors.

> The instruments of torture were shown to her, and next to them the torturers, Mauger, Leparmentier, and his assistants. Also present was the usual array of *greffiers de douleurs* and the *notaires d'angoisse*, trained in the indispensable art of picking confessions from the incomprehensible shrieks of the victims.
>
> Monsieur de Beauvais gave her sufficient time to take in the nature of the assembled implements, the pullies and cords, the winches and the rack, the mallets and the funnels, the hooks, the gridirons, the knives, the spikes, the boot, the pincers, and the braziers glowing in the shadows.

And having been thus faced with the threat of imminent torture, Joan was interrogated again, with what result we are only too familiar.

The Papal Inquisition usually subjected its accused to the *murus largus*, an ordinary prison cell, or the *murus strictus*, a small dungeon. Prisoners in the former were permitted exercise, visitors, and presents of food and clothing. But in the *murus strictus*, prisoners were chained by the ankles in dark, confined spaces, and fed through slits in the walls.

In Rome, the Pope had his own prison, in the Castel Sant'Angelo, originally the mausoleum of the Emperor Hadrian on the west bank of the Tiber. Some of the popes had come to bad ends themselves in the Castel Sant'Angelo in earlier times. In 929 Pope John X died in mysterious circumstances whilst imprisoned there. He had been deposed by the senatrix Marozia, who virtually ruled Rome at that time, and it is generally thought that she had him suffocated. Marozia herself was imprisoned in the fortress later, and in all probability died or was murdered there, as she was never heard of again. In 974 Pope Benedict VI was seized by rebels and thrown into the prison to await trial, but his successor,

Boniface VII, had him strangled in prison. And ten years later, Boniface had his rival John XIV brutally treated and thrown into gaol, and he died in Castel Sant'Angelo, either from starvation or by poison.

Pope Clement VII starved one of his prisoners to death there. Fra Benedetto da Foiano had been thrown into the worst dungeon in the castle in 1530 for preaching against the Medici family, and was left to die slowly with inadequate food and water.

Paul III imprisoned the sculptor and goldsmith Benvenuto Cellini in Sant'Angelo for 'homicides and other devilries', and then, embarrassed by the international fame of his prisoner, planned to put him to death by some means that would not arouse suspicion. Cellini, however, managed to escape, but broke his leg and was soon recaptured, and taken at first to one of Rome's worst prisons, the Torre di Nona, fearing that he was to have his throat cut. But he was returned to the Castel Sant'Angelo, and put in the charge of a mad gaoler in a dim dungeon below ground level, swarming with insects and spiders, and flooded, with only a hemp mattress between him and the drenched stone floor. The mattress quickly soaked up water. After four months in these terrible conditions, Cellini was suddenly seized by several guards, by order of the castellan, who was incensed by his prisoner's apparently unquenchable spirit. Cellini feared that he was to be thrown down the oubliette of Sammabo, a deep pit in the castle's foundations. But they put him instead in the dark dungeon where Fra Foiano had died some years earlier. Here, powdered diamond was mixed with his food, with the intention of perforating his bowels and stomach and so causing his death, but the man who had been ordered to grind the diamond to power had kept the precious stone for himself and replaced it with a substance that was less harmful. Soon afterwards, Pope Paul, drunk after a good dinner, gave in to pressure from those who wanted Cellini released.

The name of Tomás de Torquemada, the Dominican Inquisitor-General of Spain in the fifteenth century, looms over all other figures in the popular image of the Spanish Inquisition, and his hideous cruelty lends force to the notorious reputation of towns such as Madrid, Seville, Valladolid, and Toledo, the former Spanish capital and scene of Poe's story, where Jews, Protestants and Moors were regularly imprisoned, tortured and burnt alive in the main square, the Plaza de Zocodover. The prison at Las Palmas in the Canary Islands also acquired a grim reputation. Prisoners of the Spanish Inquisition were truly enemies of the state as much as enemies of the Church, for inquisitors were directly responsible to the King and Queen, Ferdinand and Isabella, rather than to the Pope.

Suspects were held for interrogation in the *cárceles secretas*, dark cells, in an atmosphere of terror. If the use of cruel torture by the Inquisition has been exaggerated by sensational writers, and long-term prisoners were as likely to die from disease as under torture, it *was* nevertheless employed extensively, and there are many records of broken limbs and the mutilation of those who did not recant as soon as they were shown the instruments. Thus we are presented with the grotesque spectacle of Dominican and Franciscan friars ordering the maiming and burning alive of their fellow human beings for the greater glory of God.

The English seaman Miles Phillips recorded his experiences as a prisoner of the Inquisition in Mexico City in 1574–5, shortly after it had been established in the Spanish colonies. A proclamation by the Chief Inquisitor, Don Pedro Moya de Contreres, forbade native Mexicans from hiding or sheltering any Englishman, and many were taken captive all over the country and conveyed to the capital, to be confined in dark dungeons for eighteen months, during which they were constantly examined about their faith. The English prisoners were all tortured on the rack, and the sentence of the Holy Inquisition was then pronounced on them. Some were burnt at the stake. Many others were whipped and condemned to serve as galley slaves for up to ten years. Phillips himself was among the fortunate ones, sentenced only to serve in a monastery for five years. But those condemned to be flogged round the city on horseback

> had the number of stripes appointed to every one of them, most cruelly laid upon their naked bodies with long whips, by sundry men appointed to be the executioners thereof . . . And all the way as they went, there were some of the Inquisitors themselves, and of the Familiars of that rakehell Order, that cried to the executioners, 'Strike! Lay on those English heretics! Lutherans! God's enemies!'
>
> So this horrible spectacle being shewed round about the city; and they returned to the Inquisitor's House, with their backs all gore blood, and swollen with greats bumps: they were then taken from their horses; and carried again to prison, where they remained until they were sent into Spain to the galleys, there to receive the rest of their martyrdom.

A Scotsman, William Lithgow, fell foul of the Inquisition at Malaga in 1620:

> I was by the executioner stripped to the skin, brought to the rack, and then mounted by him on the top of it, where soon after I was hung by the bare shoulders with two small cords, which went under both my arms, running on two rings of iron that were fixed in the wall above my head. Thus being hoisted to the appointed height, the tormentor descended below, and drawing down my legs, through the two sides of the three-planked rack, he tied a cord about each of my ankles and then ascending upon the rack he drew the cords upward, and bending forward with main force my two knees against the two planks, the sinews of my hams burst

asunder, and the lids of my knees being crushed, and the cords made fast, I hung so demained for a large hour . . .

Then the tormentor, laying the right arme above the left, and the crown upmost, did cast a cord over both arms seven distant times: and then lying down upon his back, and setting both his feet on my hollow pinched belly, he charged and drew violently with his hands, making my womb suffer the force of his feet, till the seven several cords combined in one place of my arme (and cutting the crown, sinews, and flesh to their bare bones) did pull in my fingers close to the palm of my hands; the left hand of which is lame so still and will be for ever.

These horrors were only the beginning of his sufferings, for he was subsequently racked and then subjected to the water torture, but he somehow survived and returned home after a term of imprisonment, and ignored the oath required of all released prisoners of the Inquisition that they would never reveal their experiences to anyone.

A great many towns and cities in other countries also maintained prisons that were hellholes for those whose conscience led them to deviate from the Roman faith. In France, male prisoners were often condemned to slave labour in the galleys at Toulon. One Isaac Grenier de Lasterme was condemned for life in 1753 for having 'attended religious ceremonies'. He was seventy-six years old. Marie Jaq, a widow of sixty-nine, had spent twenty-five years in prison for being 'in a society which was praying to God'.

One of the most intolerant places in Europe was the city of Toulouse, capital of Languedoc. Toulouse became known as the 'metropolis of heresy', and the Dominican convent there was called the 'Hôtel de l'Inquisition'. People were kept in prison for years on mere suspicion. One Guillem Salavert made a confession in 1299 which the Toulouse inquisitor considered unsatisfactory. He confessed again after seventeen years in prison, and was finally sentenced three years later. In 1577 four hundred supposed witches were sent to the bonfires in Toulouse.

It was in the damp and filthy dungeons of the Hôtel de Ville, the town hall, that the Huguenot tradesman Jean Calas was taken in 1761, falsely accused of murdering his son to prevent him from becoming a Roman Catholic. Marc-Antoine Calas had hanged himself, but the family concealed the facts at first because suicides in Toulouse were disgraced by being dragged through the streets to be defiled by the mob and then suspended on gibbets. M. and Mme Calas and their son Pierre were carted off to prison, and some of the judges favoured putting all three of them to torture to extract confessions. The prisoners were removed from the Hôtel de Ville to the cells of the Palais Narbonnais, where they spent eleven weeks loaded with chains in dark, foul cells which were often flooded because their floors were below the level of the River Garonne. In the event, Calas *père* alone was taken out and broken on the wheel in 1762, aged sixty-four, suffering his indescribable torments for two hours before he was mercifully strangled and his corpse burnt. Calas was the last person to be tortured and executed in this way in France, and he and his family were afterwards declared innocent after the famous campaign conducted on their behalf by Voltaire.

During the European witch-craze, the German town of Bamberg was among the most zealous in suppressing witchcraft, and one ruler, the prince-bishop Johann von Dornheim, employed full-time torturers and executioners in a building called the Hexenhaus (Witches' House), to bring these heretics to justice. He is said to have consigned six hundred supposed witches to the stake within a decade, including Johannes Junius, a burgomaster, who smuggled a letter to his daughter out of the Hexenhaus before his execution:

Innocent have I come to prison, innocent have I been

tortured, innocent must I die. For whoever comes into the witch prison must become a witch or be tortured until he invents something out of his head and – God pity him, bethinks him of something.

After putting thumbscrews on him until blood ran out at the nails, so that he could not use his hands for a month, they

first stripped me, bound my hands behind me, and drew me up in the torture. Then I thought Heaven and Earth were at an end; eight times did they draw me up and let me fall again, so that I suffered terrible agony. The executioner said: 'Sir, I beg you for God's sake confess something, whether it be true or not, for you cannot endure the torture which you will be put to, and even if you bear it at all, yet you will not escape' . . .

Now, dear child, here you have all my confession, for which I must die. And they are sheer lies and made-up things, so help me God. For all this I was forced to say through fear of the torture which was threatened beyond what I had already endured. For they never leave off with the torture till one confesses something . . .

It was a technique used widely and adapted centuries later by totalitarian states such as China and the Soviet Union. The methods of the medieval Inquisition in suppressing freedom of thought and enforcing conformity with orthodox dogma, alas, live on.

5

PETER AND PAUL FORTRESS, ST PETERSBURG

The chief state prison of the tsars of Russia, in the former
capital, was built by Peter the Great on Zayachiy Island,
on the north bank of the River Neva, in the early years of
the eighteenth century. Its appearance in this section
rather than the previous one is because it was, although
an island prison (like the moated Tower of London, for
that matter) a metropolitan fortress for prisoners of the
state rather than a place of exile isolated from centres of
civilisation. Its commencement represented the foundation of St Petersburg, and the Petropavlovsky Fortress
was intended as a bulwark against Sweden, but it was
never used in a war against a foreign power. It became,
instead, a dreaded island prison for the tsars' enemies at
home. In the two centuries of St Petersburg's ascendancy
as the capital of Russia, the fortress held some distinguished prisoners, including Dostoevsky, Gorky and
Trotsky.

Work began on the fortress in May, 1703, and was
carried out by Swedish prisoners and Russian forced
labour. The structure had six stone bastions, named
after Peter and five of his generals, and the Trubetskoi
Bastion, at the south-west corner, eventually became the
most infamous political prison in Tsarist Russia. The
Peter Gate, completed in 1718, had the double-headed
Romanov eagle above its triumphal arch. Rising above
the forbidding brown stone fortress was the golden spire
of the cathedral of SS Peter and Paul, completed in 1733,
where most of the subsequent tsars were buried. The
Commandant's House, built later, was subsequently the
scene of famous political trials, including those of the

Decembrists – aristocratic conspirators who attempted to depose Nicholas I in 1826 – and the Petrashevsky Circle in 1849.

One of the earliest prisoners here was Peter the Great's own eldest son, the twenty-eight-year-old Tsarevich Alexei. He had opposed his father's policies, and was imprisoned in 1718, having already been excluded from the line of succession. He was tried and sentenced to death, and although subsequently pardoned, it was put about that the strain of the trial resulted in his death in prison. In fact, Alexei was murdered here – beaten to death, possibly with his father's active participation.

Another who perished in the fortress's dungeons was 'Princess Tarakanov', a pretender to the throne of Russia. She tried to pass herself off as a daughter of the Empress Elizabeth, and was incarcerated here by Admiral Orlov, on behalf of Catherine the Great.

It was during Catherine's reign, in 1781, that John Howard visited the prison:

> The governor of the police at Petersburg was so kind as to fix a time for showing me all the instruments commonly used for punishment – the axe and block – the machine (now out of use) for breaking the arms and legs – the instrument for slitting or lacerating the nostrils – and that for marking criminals (which is done by punctuation, and then rubbing a black powder on the wounds – the knoot whip – and another called the cat, which consists of a number of thongs from two to ten. The knoot whip is fixed to a wooden handle a foot long, and consists of several thongs about two feet in length twisted together, to the end of which is fastened a single tough thong of a foot and a half, tapering towards a point, and capable of being changed by the executioner, when too much softened by the blood of the criminal.

Howard witnessed the punishment by the knoot whip of a man and a woman. The woman, stripped to the waist, received twenty-five lashes, and the man sixty. Howard counted the number as they were chalked on a board, noting that every stroke 'seemed to penetrate deep' into the woman's flesh.

> Both seemed but just alive, especially the man, who yet had strength enough to receive a small donation with some signs of gratitude. They were conducted back to prison in a little wagon. I saw the woman in a very weak condition some days after, but could not find the man any more.

Howard remarked that 'the common punishment of the knoot is often dreaded more than death, and sometimes a criminal has endeavoured to bribe the executioner to kill him'.

The hundred and twenty-four members of the Decembrist movement, who conspired against the authoritarian regime of Tsar Nicholas I, were tried and sentenced with precise instructions from the Tsar to the Commandant as to how each of them was to be treated in prison. Some were to be merely handcuffed, and others clapped in irons. One of the victims was to be chained 'so that he cannot move'. The five ringleaders of the conspiracy were hanged in July 1826, near the Kronverk, the northern defensive wall of the fortress, and the rest were eventually removed from the Petropavlovsky, sentenced to hard labour and banished to Siberia.

On 23 April 1849, in the early hours of the morning, Fyodor Dostoevsky, a struggling novelist in his twenties, was suddenly arrested in his lodgings in St Petersburg by Nicholas's secret police, headed by an officer in a sky-blue uniform, armed with a sabre. The young author was taken immediately to the Petropavlovsky Fortress, and confined in the dreaded Alekseyevsky Ravelin, a special prison ominously known as the 'Secret House', near the western end of the fortress.

Dostoevsky had been a member of the so-called Petrashevsky Circle, named after the political dissident

M.V. Butashevich-Petrashevsky, who led the group. It met every Friday at Petrashevsky's flat to talk rather vaguely about various matters of moment, including social reform and banned books, without making any secret of its activities. Nevertheless, it inevitably fell foul of the Tsar's paranoid fear of opposition. Thirty-four members of the circle were arrested. One of the chief members, Nikolay Speshnev, became the probable model for Dostoevsky's fascinating character Stavrogin, in *The Possessed*.

The chief charge against Dostoevsky was that he had orally disseminated a subversive document; to wit, Belinsky's open letter to Gogol. And indeed, Dostoevsky had read this social revolutionary's letter aloud to the Petrashevsky group.

Although the young Dostoevsky had strong feelings about social injustices in his country, he was a somewhat uncertain revolutionary. Even so, he was kept more or less in solitary confinement in the Peter and Paul Fortress for eight months. He suffered during this time from piles and scrofula. At first he was allowed no books or writing materials, but he made use of some of his experiences here later in *Crime and Punishment*. Interrogation resulted in twenty-three of those arrested, including the novelist, being committed for trial by a military court, which found most of them guilty of the charges against them.

On 22 December 1849, Dostoevsky and his fellow revolutionaries were taken from their dungeons and across the Neva to the city's Semyonovsky Square, where they were to be executed by firing squad. They stood for twenty minutes, stripped to their shirts in freezing weather, while the sentences were read out. Then the first three victims were tied to stakes and blindfolded.

We were bound in parties of three to stakes to suffer execution. Being third in the row, I concluded that I had only a few minutes to live. I thought of you and your dear ones, and I managed to kiss Pleshtchev and Dourov, who were next to me, and to bid them farewell.

Dostoevsky watched as the firing squad took aim, and then a messenger rode across the square with a reprieve, commuting the sentences to exile and hard labour. The whole episode had been an elaborate charade – a macabre exercise in state terrorism. The sentences had been commuted before the prisoners had left the fortress, but the Commandant had gone through with the procedure in order, no doubt, to deter the revolutionaries from ever repeating their illegal acts.

The prisoners – one of whom had gone mad under this ordeal by the time he was untied – were returned to the Petropavlovsky to be secured with fetters, and were then transported two thousand miles to Omsk. Dostoevsky described his thoughts and emotions before the firing squad in *The Idiot* and his experiences as a convict in Siberia, as we have seen, formed the basis of *Memoirs from the House of the Dead*.

Another of Dostoevsky's best-known characters – Pyotr Stepanovich Verkhovensky in *The Possessed* – was based on a notorious contemporary nihilist and terrorist, Sergei Nechaiev, a student at Moscow University. In November 1869, Nechaiev ordered the members of his fanatical revolutionary group to murder another student, named Ivan Ivanovich Ivanov, who was challenging Nechaiev's authority as self-appointed leader. After the victim had been beaten and half strangled, Nechaiev finally shot Ivanov himself, in the back of the neck, in the grounds of the Petrovsky Agricultural Academy, and he and his comrades threw the corpse, weighted with bricks, into a pond, where it was found a few days later. Dostoevsky's description of the murder of Shatov in his novel is said to be a fairly accurate representation of the killing of Ivanov. Nechaiev fled to Geneva, from where, nearly two years afterwards, the

Russian authorities managed to get him extradited, and his trial for murder began in July 1871. He was committed to the Petropavlovsky Fortress, and spent the last nine years of his life there, dying of scurvy at the age of thirty-five after two terrible years in a dungeon, into which he was thrown on discovery of his association with members of the People's Will. He did, however, manage to convert a few of his gaolers to the revolutionary cause.

The 'Secret House' of the Petropavlovsky Fortress, the Alexeyevsky Ravelin, was subsequently demolished, in 1884, after a new prison had been built in the Trubetskoi Bastion, close by, to replace the old dungeons. Some of the People's Will terrorists who assassinated Tsar Alexander II with a bomb in 1881 were held here, before being executed.

A few years later, in 1887, Alexander Ulianov was imprisoned in the Petropavlovsky, for his part in a failed conspiracy to assassinate the autocratic Tsar Alexander III. Ulianov, a student at St Petersburg University, played only a minor role in the assassination plot, but he was sentenced to death. His mother rushed to the capital from her home in Simbursk – a distance of about eight hundred miles – and made hysterical pleas for her son's life, but to no avail. Alexei was hanged. The event had a profound effect on his younger brother, Vladimir, the future Lenin, then seventeen years old.

After the events of 'Bloody Sunday' in 1905, when unarmed demonstrators were shot down by troops in front of the Winter Palace, Maxim Gorky and Leon Trotsky were among the fortress's prisoners. Gorky had sheltered the leader of the demonstrators, Father Georgi Gapon, in his flat after the massacre, and was imprisoned here for several weeks. He was incarcerated in Cell 60 of the Trubetskoi Bastion, suffering from tuberculosis and rheumatism. His temperature soared and there was international concern for his welfare. Anatole

France led an appeal from men of culture throughout Europe to save him, and under this pressure the Tsarist government set him free.

After the Revolution in 1917, there was a strong body of opinion that the former Tsar, Nicholas II, should be clapped into a bastion of the Peter and Paul Fortress until his trial and execution. This did not happen, but Anna Vyrubova, the modest intimate friend of the Tsaritsa Alexandra, was imprisoned there by the Kerensky government. Among other things, it was rumoured that she had shared the bed of both the Tsar and Rasputin, and she was put on trial for 'political activities', but a medical examination, carried out in May 1917, at her own request, proved that she was a virgin. Nevertheless, she spent five months in prison, and was rearrested later and imprisoned several times until she escaped to Finland.

In January 1919, a number of prisoners of the Bolsheviks were shot in the Peter and Paul Fortress. They included four Russian grand dukes, one of whom was the historian Nicholas Mikhailovich. Gorky pleaded with his friend Lenin to spare the life of this man, but Lenin refused, saying, 'The Revolution does not need historians.' Two years later, the trials of mutinous sailors were held in the Trubetskoi Bastion, and the condemned were shipped downriver at night to be shot or hanged at Fox Cape on the island of Kronstadt. St Petersburg had been renamed Petrograd by this time, and it was shortly to have another name – Leningrad.

The Petropavlovsky ceased to be used as a prison under the Bolsheviks, and in 1924 it was opened as a museum. Some cells were restored to their nineteenth-century appearance, and the USSR used the place for propaganda after the Second World War, to demonstrate to tourists the horrors of the tsarist regime, while the Communist authorities held thousands of prisoners in terrible conditions in the Kresty Prison, not far away, and their own chief place of horror shifted to the centre of Moscow – the equally dreaded Lubyanka.

6

THE BLACK HOLE OF CALCUTTA

Unlike most of the prisons discussed in this book, which earned their notoriety over a long period of time, the Black Hole of Calcutta bequeathed its infamous name to the history books in the course of one terrible night in 1756.

During the reign of George II, the British gradually displaced French power in India through the activities of the East India Company, an armed trading corporation. But the Nawab of Bengal, Surajah Dowlah, hated the British and found an excuse to march on the garrison of Fort William at Calcutta, with a large native army.

Five hundred men, women and children lived in this well-defended fortress of the East India Company on the bank of the Hoogly River. They thought it was impregnable, but that turned out to be wishful thinking. The Nawab's army attacked and took Calcutta. The Governor, Roger Drake, and the military commandant, Captain George Minchin, saved their own necks, making their escape by boat, and a large number of deserters fled the scene. A hundred and forty-six other British subjects were taken prisoner. All except one were men, the other being Mary Carey, a sailor's wife.

The senior person among the prisoners was John Zephaniah Holwell, the chief magistrate in Calcutta. Forty-five years old, he was a doctor as well as a lawyer, having been trained as a surgeon at Guy's Hospital. Holwell was brought before the victorious Nawab on the fortress parade ground, with his hands tied behind his back. The Nawab ordered the prisoner's hands to be released, but then spoke angrily to him, annoyed that the

British had presumed to defend the fortress with so few men. He was even more annoyed because his victory was not rewarded by the discovery of great treasure, as he had confidently expected. The Nawab ordered his men to burn down the governor's residence, but Holwell managed to extract from him a promise that the European prisoners would be well treated.

While the prisoners were being held on the parade ground, a brawl between a drunken Dutchman and one of the Nawab's soldiers resulted in the death of the soldier, and as a consequence of this the Indian officers concluded that it would not be safe to leave their prisoners in the open during the night. The Nawab was informed, and he agreed that they should be confined in the garrison's military prison cell, which was known as the 'black hole'.

Few of the prisoners knew anything about the black hole and its size, but Holwell and one or two others instantly realised the terrible implications. It was a room of about eighteen feet by fourteen, built at the end of an arcade along the east wall of Fort William. It had a low roof, one door, and two tiny windows with iron bars. It was used for confining drunken soldiers for a night – three or four at a time, at most. It was a stiflingly hot little cell, such air as there was in it foul with the stench of sweat, urine and excrement.

Into this repellent dungeon, the Indian soldiers drove their one hundred and forty-six prisoners, including a dozen wounded officers who could barely stand. Holwell was sent in first, and as the rest were ordered to follow, they thought it was some sort of joke, and laughed at the absurdity of such a crowd being shut into such a confined space. But it was no joke, and one after another the protesting and disbelieving men, and Mary Carey, were forced through the doorway at the points of swords, and the door was locked. It was the never-to-be-forgotten night of Sunday 20 June.

Crushed inside, sprawling on top of one another, struggling for space and air, the entombed prisoners pleaded for mercy with the guards outside. Some tried to break the door down. Holwell offered the soldiers large sums of money to let them out, but the Indians said they could do nothing without orders from the Nawab, who was asleep, and it was more than their lives were worth to wake him.

Even in the first minutes of their confinement, it is probable that some of the prisoners were being trampled to death in the crush. Some vomited uncontrollably at the awful stench, and in a frenzy of terror at the realisation of imminent suffocation, men hit out at their fellows in a struggle to reach the windows. The normally atrocious heat in the cell was made far worse by the mass of humanity in it and by the flames of burning buildings outside.

Although Surajah Dowlah was feared for his cruelty, there is no evidence that he intended a massacre when he ordered the prisoners to be confined in the black hole. He was not familiar with it, and he had merely taken the advice of his officers. But *they* knew perfectly well that they were condemning their prisoners to death.

Animal instincts took over most of the prisoners as they fought, raving and delirious, for survival. Some slashed at others with their pocket knives as they struggled for air and water. Several attempts were made to force the door open, but it opened inwards, and having nothing but their hands to work with, the prisoners' efforts were doomed to failure. Holwell, who had managed to keep a firm grip on one of the iron bars in a window, realised that the only hope for them was to avoid panic and keep calm, and shouted for quiet. At length he managed to subdue the screams of terror and agony enough to beg them all, for their own sakes, to preserve their energy during the night in the knowledge that the morning would bring them liberty. Even as he spoke, however, Holwell knew their chances of survival were slender.

Some men were already dead within an hour of the cell door being shut on them. As well as those who had been trampled or had sunk to the ground through suffocation, a few dead were still standing up, crushed so tightly by their neighbours that their bodies could not collapse. Someone suggested that there would be a little more space if everyone took their clothes off, and most of the prisoners struggled to strip. Some who had hats began to fan themselves, and soon a large number of hats was being waved frantically to produce some circulation of air in the cell.

As the various remedies failed to relieve the situation, however, blind panic again took over. Some prisoners, choking and gasping for breath, begged the guards to open fire and put them out of their misery. They fought like savages for water when one of the more sympathetic guards filled felt hats stretched out at the windows. Other guards came to watch the curiosity of Englishmen fighting like animals for a drop of water, and held lights up to the bars, the better to see a scene that was like something out of Dante's *Inferno*. Holwell later described the terrible ordeal, in a letter to a friend which was never intended for publication, but which became our chief source of knowledge about the night's events.

> Oh! my dear Sir, how shall I give you a conception of what I felt at the cries and ravings of those in the remoter part of the prison, who could not entertain a probable hope of obtaining a drop, yet could not divest themselves of expectation, however unavailing . . . Several quitted the other window (the only chance they had for life) to force their way to the water, and the throng and press upon the window was beyond bearing; many forcing their passage from the further part of the room, pressed down those in their way, who had less strength, and trampled them to death.

Holwell, refusing to release his grip on the iron bar, was almost pressed to death himself, and his legs nearly broken with the weight against them. He was aware, when he was able to shift his weight from one foot to the other, that he was standing on the faces of dead men. He considered opening his veins with his pocket knife, and already had the knife out and poised when he changed his mind.

Men desperate for moisture licked the perspiration from their bodies, or drank their own urine. Holwell admitted afterwards that 'in an ungovernable fit of thirst' he had 'attempted drinking my urine; but it was so intensely bitter, there was no enduring a second taste . . .' He then sucked the perspiration from the sleeves of his shirt.

As more men died, they afforded the living the slight relief of a little more space to move, though it was only on top of fresh corpses. Holwell saw the sailor Carey die in the arms of his wife. She, being a half-caste, seemed better able than the English to tolerate the appalling conditions. Holwell himself then lost consciousness.

As dawn approached, two of the survivors found Holwell's body, and at first thought he was dead, but as he showed signs of life they dragged him to a window to show him to the soldiers outside, knowing that the Nawab would not want the magistrate dead, for Surajah Dowlah, convinced that the garrison had hidden its treasure, believed that Holwell alone knew its where-abouts. Holwell's survival was undoubtedly due to the fact that, being first into the cell, he had taken up a position at one of the windows and refused to be shifted from it.

When the Nawab was informed by one of his officers that the life of the magistrate could be saved only if the black hole were opened immediately, he ordered it to be done, and at six o'clock the key was turned to release the prisoners. But the weight of dead bodies against the door prevented the guards from pushing it open. The first thing to burst out of the room when the door was pushed slightly was the sickening stench of death, sweat and urine. The surviving prisoners had to drag away the corpses of their comrades before they could get out. When that was done, twenty-two men and Mary Carey staggered out of the black hole, and lay for a time gasping on the parade ground, while the ruins of Fort William still smouldered around them. Inside the charnel house were left the bodies of a hundred and twenty-three dead who had expired in the course of ten hours since the door had been locked on them.

Indian soldiers took the dead away on carts, and buried them in a ditch, helping themselves to any property they thought worth taking, such as shoes and rings. All the survivors were allowed to leave, except Holwell and three other men who were clapped in irons because Holwell could not tell the Nawab where to find the non-existent treasure. They were kept prisoner for three more weeks before they, too, were finally released.

Calcutta was soon retaken by an army of British infantry and Indian sepoys under the command of Robert Clive, and Clive's famous victory at Plassey, twelve months after the night of the Black Hole, sealed the fate of India for the best part of two hundred years, Calcutta becoming the capital of British India.

The commercial centre of modern Calcutta stands on the site of the old Fort William, and the Black Hole stood near what is now the General Post Office.

7

SING SING, NEW YORK

Sing Sing Prison is about thirty miles north of New York City, on the east bank of the Hudson River at Ossining, in Westchester County. When the prison, originally called 'Mount Pleasant', was built, in 1824–5, the town itself was known as Sing Sing, from the Indian *sint sinks* – 'stone upon stone' – a name it retained until 1901.

The prison was planned to replace New York's 'Newgate' at Greenwich Village. Its site was chosen to take advantage of convict labour to quarry the local marble, which was then being used extensively for the neo-classical buildings rising in New York. A hundred prisoners were brought to the site, shackled, with thirty armed guards, to carry out labour under expert supervision, and the prison gradually rose from its rocky foundations, the men working in silence. When it was completed, it had a thousand cells, each seven feet by three and a half feet, and six feet high. The population of Newgate was transferred there, and by 1830, there were eight hundred prisoners.

The prison was based on the Auburn system, then the latest model in American penal institutions. This had in turn replaced the famous Pennsylvania separate system of solitary confinement, devised by the Quakers, which had been found to lead to a considerable increase in insanity and suicide. The Auburn silent system was based on separate confinement at night, with a prohibition on conversation during the day. The new prison's regime was a harsh one. Not only were the inmates not allowed to speak to one another, but they were allowed no visitors and no mail. They were confined in their cells from Saturday noon until Monday morning, and during the week shuffled about their business in chains and their striped convict uniforms. The unhealthy old cell-block, with no modern ventilation or central heating system, was like an oven in the summer months and an ice-box in winter.

Sing Sing's symbol of authority was the cat-o'-nine-tails. One offender against the rules died under the lash. Other punishments included beatings with the 'paddle' – a leather weapon shaped like a canoe paddle; cold-water showers, confinement in dark cells, and various forms of restriction of movement, such as ball and chain, and the 'cage' – an iron collar padlocked round the prisoner's neck with iron bars or prongs projecting upward from it to enclose the head.

By 1859, the new prison was already overcrowded, and two men were sharing many of the tiny cells, 1,600 men being confined in a building meant to accommodate up to 1,200. This situation was discontinued in 1912, largely to control homosexual practices. Until 1877, up to two hundred women could also be accommodated at Sing Sing, in a separate block, but after this date, the only women prisoners here were those under sentence of death.

The suicide rate in the prison was high, and not surprisingly, escape attempts were frequent right from the start. In 1877 a twenty-foot-high wall was built round the prison, with armed observation posts. But many prisoners thought the risk of being shot trying to get away was better than suffering under the cat. One convict was shot after attacking a warder. The sounds of sirens and gunfire became almost routine accompaniments to life in the neighbourhood.

The administration of Sing Sing was appalling in the early years. When a professional accountant was called in to carry out an enquiry into the prison economy, he found discrepancies between the prison registers and the actual number of inmates. There were only 762 men in the prison, though the books showed 795; and 82 women, though the books showed 102. More than fifty missing prisoners were virtually written off like bad debts. There were similar serious discrepancies with the prison accounts.

Many wardens resigned after very short experiences during the first half-century of Sing Sing's existence. The average length of service was less than a year, and it was a standard joke among the prisoners that the quickest way to get out of Sing Sing was to come in as warden.

The early horrors of Sing Sing are brought home to us in the accounts of the insane who were sometimes wrongly committed to the prison, and of the desperate drug addicts who would make half-inch slits in their own flesh and pack the wounds with a cheap opium residue known as 'eng shee', until the traces of opiate were absorbed into their bloodstreams. Their wounds then resulted in severe abscesses.

Gradually the harshness of life in Sing Sing was relaxed under increasingly progressive regimes. Prisoners were allowed to receive visitors once in six months, and the state legislature abolished – in theory – all punishments except the dark cell. In practice, however, things improved only slowly and a little at a time. During the course of 1873, seventy-two men were strung up by their thumbs in a dark cell, with their toes only just touching the ground. In the following year, a prisoner named Appo was beaten unconscious for accidentally scorching a shirt he was ironing. He then threw the rest of the shirts in his pile into a stove, and was locked up in a dark cell for two weeks and allowed only bread and water. A prisoner named Thompson was shot dead for speaking to his neighbour in a workshop.

Two men, named Pallister and Roehl, escaped from the condemned cells in April 1893, where they were both awaiting execution for separate murders. They made their escape during a violent storm, and were never recaptured. It was assumed that they had drowned whilst trying to cross the Hudson River in a small boat in appalling conditions, but that is not known for certain.

By the end of the century, Sing Sing had been condemned as an unsanitary building with inadequate facilities, but it was not until 1920 that a new prison was begun on a hill overlooking the old one and linked to it. By this time, guided tours were allowed round a place which had become as famous – throughout the United States and beyond – as the Statue of Liberty. The additional buildings included new cell-blocks, an administration building and a hospital, and the prison was run like a factory, with prisoners making shoes and articles of clothing, flags and brushes and other items, for sale outside. Under an enlightened system, Sing Sing was no longer the hellhole it had been during the nineteenth century for prisoners doing long stretches with no hope of parole.

By this time, however, Sing Sing Prison had become notorious for a different reason. In August 1890, the first execution by means of electricity had been carried out at Auburn State Prison, and it was not long before an electric chair was installed at Sing Sing. The first victim of this new method of execution at Sing Sing died on 7 July 1891. Eight years later, the first woman to be electrocuted in New York State died at Sing Sing on 20 March 1899. She was Martha Place, who had been convicted of the murder of her stepdaughter and the attempted murder of her husband.

The first electrical executioner was one Davis, the technician at Auburn Prison, who retained his position there and came to Sing Sing whenever his services were required. He was succeeded by his former assistant, Hilbert, who eventually committed suicide.

As with most methods of execution, the electric chair was less than perfect, especially in its early years. A man named Taylor had had to be dosed with anaesthetics for more than an hour at Auburn, in July 1893, when a fault was found with the chair after he had been strapped into it. In the early years of the twentieth century, Antonio Ferrarea needed seven jolts of 1,400 volts to be administered before the prison doctor pronounced him dead. A doctor who had to witness a hundred and thirty-eight executions during his years at Sing Sing wrote that '. . . neither I nor any of the wardens I ever knew could force ourselves to sleep at all on the night of an electrocution. The strain upon us was too intense.'

Once seven men were executed in one day – five of them for the same murder. Some of the condemned were Italian immigrants, who shrieked and moaned as they awaited their turns. Their friends and relatives were allowed to take their bodies away after their deaths, and the corpses were exhibited in Brooklyn for a time, an admission fee being charged, until public health officers put an end to this macabre practice.

Since 1916 all executions in New York State have been carried out at Sing Sing. The prison's new death house consisted of twenty-four cells for condemned men and three for women. This special wing of the prison had its own hospital, kitchen and visiting room. There were six cells in the pre-execution chamber, known to inmates as the 'dance hall', and adjacent to the execution chamber itself was a morgue, known as the 'ice-house'. Executions were carried out, as a rule, at eleven o'clock on Thursday nights, and those condemned to die would be moved on the morning of their executions to cells adjacent to the execution chamber.

When a prisoner was sentenced to death, there would normally be a six-month interval between the sentence and its confirmation by the State Court of Appeals. This period of mental torture was spent in the death-house wing of the prison. At the time of execution, a male prisoner would have one of his trouser legs slit to the knee by a guard in his cell. Then he would be marched the short distance to the execution chamber, where a number of officially approved witnesses would already be seated to witness the execution. The prisoner would be strapped by his arms, legs and torso into the heavy oak chair, and an electrode attached to his leg. A mask of leather would then be placed over his face, and a skull cap fitted, containing a cathode element. The executioner would then switch on the current at an instrument panel behind the chair. As two thousand volts shot through the victim's body, it would lurch forward in a fearful convulsion, straining at the straps, the neck and hands turning scarlet, and the smell of burning flesh accompanying the wisp of smoke rising from the head.

When the droning current was switched off, after a few seconds, the prison doctor would apply a stethoscope to the victim's chest, and if he were still alive, the operation would be repeated. Two shocks were nearly always sufficient to kill the victim. The body would then be released and taken to the morgue for an autopsy.

The heart of an electrocuted criminal becomes dilated and filled with fluid blood, and the lungs are generally engorged with blood, which goes a dark brown colour. The lenses in the eyes have star fractures. The law on autopsies after execution required that the top of the victim's skull should be removed and the brain examined, and at one time, other men in the condemned cells could hear the dead man's skull being sawn off in the nearby 'ice-house'. This naturally caused a great deal of mental agony, and sometimes hysteria, in those whose turn was yet to come.

Among the women who came to Sing Sing's execution chamber was Ruth Snyder, along with her lover Judd Gray. They had doped, battered and strangled Albert Snyder, after she had insured her husband's life for a hundred thouand dollars. Labelled by reporters the 'granite woman', because of her persistent determination to kill her husband, Snyder was conducted to the electric chair in January 1928. One of the witnesses had smuggled a camera into the execution chamber, and took a blurred photograph of Ruth Snyder in her death throes. This was made possible because a female guard, who had been standing in a position to shield Snyder from the gathered audience, collapsed with emotion just at the fatal moment. Thereafter, execution witnesses were always searched before admission to the chamber. The only female *witness* allowed in to Sing Sing was so overcome by the awful proceeding that she had to be carried out.

A few years later, in July 1936, New York's so-called 'Borgia Killer', Mrs Creighton, was unconscious when she was lifted into the electric chair and executed. Earlier that year, Sing Sing was the scene of Albert Fish's execution. Sentenced for the murder of ten-year-old Grace Budd, he was believed to have murdered fifteen children, and was a self-confessed cannibal. He had cut up Grace Budd's body and eaten parts of it with boiled carrots and onions.

In 1944, Louis 'Lepke' Buchalter, commonly known as 'the judge', was electrocuted at Sing Sing. He was one of the originators of the notorious 'Syndicate' or 'Murder Incorporated', and was labelled by the FBI at the time as 'the most dangerous criminal in the United States'. Buchalter's mob of gunmen had killed an indeterminate number of people in the Depression years and after, but he was only brought to book because one of his assassins turned informer when arrested. Buchalter was convicted of the murder of Joe Rosen, a garment industry trucker whom he had forced out of business in 1932 and then killed to prevent him from talking. Buchalter is the only top mobster in organised crime to have been legally executed in America.

Further notoriety surrounded Sing Sing with the

execution of the spies Julius and Ethel Rosenberg in June 1953. Ten witnesses watched, and reported to the world, as Julius, first into the chair, had to be given three doses of current, lasting three, fifty-seven and fifty-seven seconds, before he was pronounced dead. Then the horrified witnesses saw Ethel's violent contractions as she was given five shocks before her life was pronounced extinct.

Claims are still made, nevertheless, that execution in the electric chair produces instantaneous death, and this is the method still used by many of the states that retain the death penalty.

8

LUBYANKA, MOSCOW

After the Bolshevik Revolution of 1917, the former Russian capital, St Petersburg, was displaced as the seat of government by Moscow, the ancient capital of Muscovy. Along with the new rulers came the All-Russian Extraordinary Commission for Combating Counter-Revolution and Sabotage, better known as 'Cheka' – the state's new secret police. This organisation established its headquarters in the former offices of the Rossiya Insurance Company. The large building stood at a corner of the Lubyanskaya Ploschad, about a kilometre north-east of the Kremlin. Since then, the name of the square has been changed to Ploschad Dzerzhinskogo, after the founder of Cheka, the Polish Bolshevik Feliks Dzerzhinsky. The occupants of the building have also undergone changes of title several times – to the GPU in 1922; the OGPU in 1923; the NKVD in 1934; the MVD in 1946; and, finally, the KGB in 1954. But the building's function has remained the same – the headquarters of the secret police and a state prison for political prisoners. And the building, though much altered and extended over the years, still goes under the name given to it in 1918 and since notorious throughout the world – the Lubyanka.

The original building was a pre-revolutionary Gothic block. During the 1930s some extension was carried out in the contemporary functional style, and after the Second World War further extensions were built, until the whole area had been converted into a network of offices and cells. From the time of the NKVD (the People's Commissariat for Internal Affairs), offices occupied the whole outer section of the complex. Inside there was a courtyard, within which stood the prison section. This had originally been a hotel run by the insurance company. Now its rooms were converted to cells, with their large windows retained, so that on the face of it, the hundred and fifty cells were not as unpleasant as those of most prisons. But the windows were blocked by shutters known as 'Yezhov muzzles' during the NKVD period. They left only a glimpse of sky visible from the inside. And although the corridors were kept clean, and smelled of disinfectant and carbolic soap, the cells, especially those in the cellar or basement, were often dirty and bug-ridden holes, freezing during the winter months and stiflingly hot in summer. Prisoners' clothing would become damp and their bread mouldy.

During this period, prisoners in the Lubyanka were not allowed books and they were not permitted to communicate with one another. When warders were escorting prisoners along corridors, they gave advance warning to others of their approach, with clicking sounds made with their tongues or their belt-buckles, so that other prisoners in the corridors could be turned to face the walls. No prisoner was allowed to recognise anyone outside his own cell.

Prisoners punished for even minor offences would be deprived of half their rations and made to stand all day in their underwear. They were allowed to lie down on the stone floors at night. There was one basement cell, about fifteen feet square, known as the 'kennel'. Sixty men were sometimes packed into it for a week or more. Its only ventilation was via the narrow gap under the door. Prisoners there invariably suffered from nausea, eczema or palpitations.

It was not for these unpleasant inconveniences, however, that Muscovites in the thirties, as Malcolm Muggeridge noted, quickened their steps and dropped their voices as they passed within the shadows of the building. They knew that here, only a few minutes' walk from the Bolshoi Theatre, dissidents were tortured and liquidated. It was said that when capital punishment had been formally abolished in the Soviet Union in 1920, Cheka men had hurriedly shot about a hundred and sixty prisoners in the yard.

Stalin's 'Great Purge' of 1936–8 was carried out by the infamous head of the NKVD, Nikolay Yezhov, who issued orders from his office here for the execution of dissidents. Stalin's excuse for a massive pogrom had been provided by the assassination of the Leningrad party boss, Sergei Kirov, and it is suspected that Stalin engineered the killing himself in order to create a pretext for the purge. Thousands of arrests were made, and those held were intimidated or tortured into confessing that they had been involved in a conspiracy to kill Stalin, or overthrow the Soviet system, or promote capitalism. The victims accused by Stalin of being 'enemies of the working class' and 'betrayers of the motherland' included artists and intellectuals, Communist Party officials, trade union leaders, Red Army generals, members of the Politburo, diplomats, and many others. Those condemned to death were often shot the same day, and the Lubyanka was the scene of many of the executions. Among the first victims were Zinoviev and Kamenev, shot within twenty-four hours of their sentences.

Karl Steiner was an Austrian who had lived in Yugoslavia for many years and had adopted the Serbo-Croat form of his name, Karlo Štajner, but had fled from Yugoslavia to the USSR to escape the persecution of Communists. He was arrested in Moscow in November 1936, by NKVD officers who came to his apartment at three o'clock in the morning. He was taken to the Lubyanka and put into a room with many others. After waiting for two hours, he was taken out and searched thoroughly, then led along corridors to a stinking cell about ten by sixteen feet, where between thirty and forty men were lying on the bare floor with a *parasha* – a latrine bucket. One of these men had been there for four months without a hearing. It was like a nightmare invented by Kafka. Most of the men were unaware of why they had been arrested and had no idea what charges were to be brought against them. They called the room *sobachnik* ('the doghouse'). They were fed on black bread and water.

Eventually, Štajner was taken up to the second floor, then down into a courtyard, into another building and up to the fifth floor. Here he was accused of belonging to a counter-revolutionary movement responsible for the assassination of Kirov, and of being an agent of the Gestapo. He laughed and denied it, and was taken back to the cell. Later he was transferred to another cell, with iron beds, straw sacks, and sheets and pillows. He was allowed fifteen minutes' exercise a day, walking round with other prisoners in single file with their hands behind their backs. They were fed with black bread for breakfast, soup and peas for lunch, and gruel for dinner.

Štajner was interrogated every day for nearly two weeks. He was shown the warrant for his arrest, signed by Andrei Vyshinsky, Commissar for Justice. At first, he was interrogated in a polite and formal manner, and pressed to sign a confession. But as he consistently refused, his interrogators lost patience, shouting and banging their fists on the desk. After about six weeks, he was transferred to the Butyrki Fortress, the largest NKVD prison in Moscow, and later to the Lefortovo, before being sent to the Siberian labour camps.

The Polish prisoner Stypulkowski described the common feeling of the accused in these places as they were led to interrogation:

This journey itself was menacing. Everything contributed to make it so; the hands bent to the back, the gloomy behaviour of the silent guard, the dark, empty corridors, the wire netting on the staircase, the rhythm of the movements and the echo of smacking lips. It stimulated imagination as to what would happen to me in a few minutes' time. Where were they taking me, and what for? The staging played an important part in the methods of inquest which were applied to me. It remained suggestive until the last day, although, after many migrations of this kind, I knew, like a well-broken horse, where I should have to turn my face to the wall, and whether the guards gripped my right or left arm.

General Iona Yakir was an army commander and member of the Central Committee of the Communist Party. Yakir, who was Jewish, was charged with working for Nazi Germany, as well as with Trotskyite terrorism. Arrested by NKVD officers in May 1937, he was driven to Moscow at high speed and thrown into a solitary cell in the Lubyanka, after his medals and chevrons had been torn from his uniform. When he wrote to assure the Politburo of his loyalty, Stalin scribbled on his letter, 'Scoundrel and prostitute', and his fate was sealed. One of Stalin's henchman wrote on his papers, 'For the traitor ... one punishment – the death sentence'. Several days of interrogation and beatings secured a 'confession' from Yakir. He was shot in June, reputedly in the yard of the Lubyanka to the accompaniment of revved-up motor engines. Later, his wife, brother and other relatives were also liquidated.

It is said that the engines of stationary lorries were customarily revved up when executions were being carried out, indoors or out, to drown any sounds that might otherwise be heard beyond the prison walls. Warders and NKVD officers would appear at the cell doors of the condemned, who would be taken to the death cell wearing only their underclothes. The NKVD's executioners, often drunk or doped with cocaine, would shoot their victims through the backs of their heads with

TT automatic weapons. This method was calculated to render the faces of the corpses unrecognisable. Execution with a small-bore pistol is not a humane way of killing. A large proportion of those shot needed a second bullet to finish them off. The prison doctor would sign the death certificates, and the naked bodies would be taken out for burial in the Kalivnikovskoye Cemetery in the middle of the night, with rags stuffed into the bullet holes in their heads. A woman was employed full time at the Lubyanka to wash the bloody tarpaulin on the floor of the execution chamber.

Many prisoners whose response to preliminary interrogation in the Lubyanka was unsatisfactory to the authorities – as in Stajner's case – were transferred to the Lefortovo Prison, which had an even worse reputation inside Russia than the Lubyanka. Torture was practised as a matter of course there, and corpses brought out under cover of darkness were ominously cremated.

The method of interrogation we have come to know as 'brainwashing' was, one account says,

> proudly referred to by the officials of the NKVD as the Yeshov method, [and] consisted of making it the arrested man's primary task to build up the whole case against himself . . . The grotesque result of this was that the accused strained every nerve to convince their examining magistrates that their invented 'legends' were true and represented the most serious crimes possible.

It was common practice for interrogators to fire the same question at a stubborn prisoner for hours on end until he was falling almost unconscious from the ordeal of denying the accusation repeatedly and struggling against falling into the trap of saying whatever was required of him, for the sake of some respite. Stypulkowski described a friend and fellow-prisoner who had been interrogated for two months:

> I could hardly recognise him. His eyes were restless and

wild, sunk deep in his skull. His skin was yellow and wrinkled and covered thickly with sweat. The face of this skeleton was spotted. His body was incessantly shaking . . .

Stalin's paranoia eventually led to suspicion of the NKVD itself. On 18th March 1937, Yezhov addressed senior officers in the Lubyanka club-room, prior to an internal purge in which three thousand officers were executed. Many others committed suicide, some throwing themselves to their deaths in the Moscow streets from their office windows on the building's upper floors. Yezhov himself then fell from power, to be replaced as the new boss of the Lubyanka by Lavrenty Beria. No one was sure for many years what had happened to Yezhov. Stories that he had gone mad were probably only propaganda to throw blame on him for some of the NKVD's known excesses. Some said he had hanged himself. In fact, he was shot in 1940, after being accused of plotting to kill Stalin and seize power, and of being a British spy.

Beria introduced some minor reforms to the Lubyanka. Inmates were allowed to read books, for instance, though the library consisted mainly of volumes which had been confiscated from prisoners. Breakfast consisted of tea and dry bread; lunch, a ladle of soup and a ladle of thin gruel.

Such was the state of Stalin's mind that in October 1941, senior Soviet officers were being severely tortured and then shot in the Lubyanka whilst inexperienced lieutenants were commanding Red Army battalions in the desperate war against Hitler. Among the victims were three successive heads of the Soviet Air Force. The period was truly akin to a Kafkaesque nightmare, people finding themselves in Lubyanka cells without knowing why they had been arrested.

When Alexander Solzhenitsyn was arrested and taken to the Lubyanka in February 1945, he was conducted to a tiny basement cell so small that he could not lie down in it. Its furniture consisted only of a table and a stool. A two-hundred-watt light bulb hung from the ceiling. After a short time, Solzhenitsyn was taken to another room where he was ordered to strip naked, and he was subjected to a thorough and intimate body search. When his clothes had been thoroughly searched as well, he was left alone and got dressed. Then a warder came in and ordered him to undress again and sit on a stool. The warder then, without uttering a word, shaved the prisoner's head, his armpits and his pubic hair. Finally, Solzhenitsyn was given a medical examination before being returned to his tiny cell.

Hardly had he settled back into this box before he was again taken out and given a shower and issued with prison clothing. Back in his cell, he was yet again shortly removed, this time to be photographed and finger-printed. When all these proceedings were complete, Solzhenitsyn was at last left in his cell, but he was not allowed to sleep, being constantly roused by warders who had told him to stay awake. The bright light was, in any case, never switched off.

Then he was again ordered out, and led to different cells, down stairs, along corridors and up in lifts, until he ended up thoroughly disorientated in a bare but larger cell which turned out to be a place of solitary confine-ment during his interrogation, which took place in one of the opulent offices of the former insurance company. Solzhenitsyn was accused of anti-Soviet propaganda and founding an organisation hostile to the state. The practice was to forbid prisoners to sleep during daylight hours and then interrogate them during the night, often until dawn, so that, numbed by lack of sleep, they were confused and vulnerable. The obtaining of confessions was the primary object of interrogation, or failing that, the accumulation of sufficient 'evidence', whether true or false, to convict prisoners of the 'crimes' they were charged with.

After a few days, Solzhenitsyn was removed to a cell with three other prisoners, one of whom was a specially planted stool-pigeon, indulged by the authorities as long as he reported to them in detail what his cell-mates said and the state of their morale. During this stage of his confinement, Solzhenitsyn was allowed twenty minutes a day for fresh air and exercise, which he took in a concrete-walled yard on the Lubyanka roof. He could hear the traffic far below as he walked round with his hands behind his back, which was compulsory.

After Stalin's death in 1953, Beria, the odious and sycophantic head of the police whose organisation was by then called the MVD (Ministry of the Interior), fell from grace at once, and was arrested. Beria had been Stalin's chief henchman in the repressive techniques of the Soviet regime, as Himmler was Hitler's in the Nazi organisation. He was responsible to Stalin for organising the assassination of Trotsky in Mexico; for administering the notorious Gulag labour camps; and was possibly over-zealous in interpreting Stalin's orders to close three prisoner-of-war camps as meaning the liquidation of fifteen thousand Polish officers, who were systematically shot at Katyn Forest and elsewhere.

Some suspect that Stalin was assassinated, and if so, Beria is the chief suspect. It was announced in December 1953, at any rate, that Beria had been executed, and it is believed that he was shot in the cellars of the Lubyanka – a classic case of the biter bit. Shortly afterwards, the Lubyanka's tenants got another new title, the KGB (Committee of State Security).

One of the enduring mysteries of the Lubyanka concerns the fate of Raoul Wallenberg, the Swedish diplomat who saved many thousands of Hungarian Jews from the Nazis by issuing them with Swedish passports and placing them in protected houses in Budapest. When the Red Army marched into Budapest in January 1945, Wallenberg was arrested, and disappeared into Stalin's camps. Persistent protests from Sweden eventually drew a statement from the Soviet authorities that Wallenberg was dead. According to the Foreign Minister, Andrei Gromyko, he died in the Lubyanka on 16 July 1947. But there were reports as late as the 1970s that Wallenberg had been seen alive.

Greville Wynne, the British agent arrested by the KGB in 1962, confirmed much of what Solzhenitsyn had experienced in the Lubyanka. Wynne described how he was taken to his cell in a steel lift with a spring-lock on the door. He was not permitted to lie down during the daytime. The guards wore slippers, so that prisoners could not hear them approaching, as they paraded round two floors of twenty-eight cells each, surrounding a rectangular hall. Wynne, too, lived at first on a diet of tea, soup and black bread, and was subjected to the same intimate body search, while women looked on, laughing, as blood ran down his legs from the rough technique of the search. He, too, was allowed his daily exercise in a walled pen on the building's flat roof. There were several such pens, with barbed wire on the tops of the high walls, and a raised wooden platform where guards stood, armed with tommy-guns.

A statue of Dzerzhinsky still stood in the square outside the building until, after the coup fiasco of August 1991, demonstrators managed to topple 'Iron Feliks', as he was known, from his plinth. *Perestroika* and the reform of the KGB have now led to some limited filming inside the Lubyanka's more respectable rooms and offices, taking away just a little of the building's air of menace. Because of the prison's original function, its rooms have a less unpleasant look than those of purpose-built prisons. But it will probably be a long time before ordinary Russians can pass this monument to state terrorism without a shiver of apprehension.

9

SPANDAU, BERLIN

Spandau is one of Berlin's western suburbs. The prison there was originally built in 1876 as a military fortress. It could accommodate nearly six hundred prisoners. Its architecture was characteristic of the period. The entrance, on Wilhelmstrasse, was through a battlemented gatehouse with twin turrets, behind which rose a fortress-like building of red brick with castellated parapets. The prison was surrounded by walls thirty feet high.

Spandau had been an unexceptional city gaol until 1933. Then it had been utilised by the Nazis as a clearing station for prisoners bound for concentration camps. Many victims of the Gestapo were executed there, often by strangulation after being hanged on short ropes from iron hooks. The prison's execution chamber had a guillotine, which was still there when the Allies took over Spandau in 1947. The floor was sloped so that blood could be drained off it. Capital punishment had been abolished by the Weimar Republic, but was reintroduced by Hitler. (It was abolished again by the Federal German Republic in 1949.)

After the end of the Second World War, and the International Military Tribunal at Nuremberg, Spandau was commandeered by the Allies as a prison for the seven top Nazi war criminals who had been spared the death penalty and sentenced to terms of imprisonment ranging from ten years to life. The occupying powers were engaged in lengthy disputes and negotiations, for months after the Nuremberg sentences were announced, about where the Nazi prisoners were to be detained, and finally agreed on Spandau, which stood in the British sector of occupied Berlin. The former German capital lay behind the so-called Iron Curtain, and was administered by a quadripartite Allied 'Kommandatura'. Throughout almost the duration of the Cold War, even at its most tense and acrimonious, the running of Spandau was one thing in which the Soviet Union and the western Allies had to co-operate on a daily basis.

The seven prisoners who arrived at Spandau on 18 July 1947, and who were henceforth to be known to prison staff by numbers only, were:

No. 1: Baldur von Schirach, the Hitler Youth leader and later Gauleiter of Vienna, sentenced to twenty years.

No. 2: Grand Admiral Karl Dönitz, the Führer's appointed successor, sentenced to ten years.

No. 3: Baron Konstantin von Neurath, Hitler's first Foreign Minister, and Reichsprotektor of Bohemia and Moravia prior to the notorious Heydrich. Sentenced to fifteen years.

No. 4: Grand Admiral Erich Raeder, who had carried out submarine warfare against unarmed merchant shipping. Sentenced to life imprisonment.

No. 5. Albert Speer, Hitler's Minister of War Production, responsible for employing slave labour. Sentenced to twenty years.

No. 6: Walther Funk, Minister of Economics and President of the Reichsbank; guardian of gold teeth and other valuables stolen from Jewish victims of the Holocaust. Sentenced to life.

No. 7: Rudolf Hess, Deputy Führer, sentenced to life.

Their ages on arrival at Spandau ranged from Schirach's forty-one years to von Neurath's seventy-five.

The security arrangements under which these prisoners were to be held was of the highest calibre, and were enveloped in military secrecy. The bare individual cells flanked an inner cell-block corridor protected by a steel door. Each cell was about nine feet square and twelve feet high, with walls, nearly two feet thick, painted green and cream, and a whitewashed ceiling. It contained a bed, a chair and a small table, a small cupboard for clothing, etc., and a toilet. Each cell had one barred window.

The prisoners were kept in solitary confinement, except for one hour a day when they were allowed communal fresh air and exercise, but were not permitted to speak to one another. They were allowed to receive one visitor every two months. Hess refused visits from his wife and son for many years, protecting himself from the emotional impact such visits would have on his arrogant aloofness from the new world around him. Deluding himself that he was still of some account in Germany, he refused to let anyone he cared about see Adolf Hitler's former deputy in captivity like a common criminal.

The prisoners were given work to do, such as cleaning the prison and making envelopes, every day except Sunday. When they were out of their cells each day for work, exercise, baths or medical attention, the cells were searched thoroughly. Great care was taken to ensure that nothing afforded any opportunity for a prisoner to commit suicide. Even the original glass in the windows was replaced with celluloid. There were prescribed punishments for offences committed by the prisoners. They could include 'cutting off of light in the cell for a period of up to four weeks; reducing of food which will be replaced by bread and water; deprivation of furniture and clothing; and, in special cases, fettering'.

Eventually these harsh conditions were relaxed, except during the months when the Russians were in charge. The USSR's deputation always went rigorously by the book. Subsequently, however, the prisoners were allowed to work in the prison garden, growing produce for the kitchen.

Between the outer cell-block and the oval boundary walls was a cobbled courtyard. Beyond it the perimeter wall had six machine-gun posts round it. There was also a ten-foot-high fence of barbed wire, reinforced by an electrified barrier with a charge of four thousand volts. The prison's own power station made it independent of Berlin's electricity supply. Notices in German and English outside the prison warned the curious not to approach the fence – 'Guards have orders to shoot'. There was much concentration on keeping the unwanted out, as well as the wanted in. There were one or two alleged plots, over the years, to free the prisoners, particularly Hess.

Spandau became known as the world's best-guarded prison. Its seven inmates were the responsibility of over a hundred staff – soldiers, warders, maintenance staff, cooks, laundresses, as well as four medical officers and the four prison directors, one British, one French, one American, one Russian. The four powers took it in turns, a month at a time, to supply the military personnel and the professional prison staff in charge of the inner cell-block.

The cost of running the prison was thus extremely high, and Berlin had also lost one of its best civil jails. There were proposals at one stage to separate the prisoners by handing them over to the countries whose troops had captured them. This would have left the Russians with only Raeder. The idea came to nothing.

There was a constant campaign, carried out mainly by the wives and lawyers of the prisoners, to ease their conditions of confinement, and to have them released. Appeals were made on behalf of the prisoners to the Pope, the Archbishop of Canterbury, and Winston Churchill. But even when the western Allies were willing to discuss remission of any of the sentences, the Soviet

Union always vetoed such proposals, until the end of 1954.

On 6 November of that year, von Neurath was released, on humanitarian grounds, having served nine of his fifteen years' sentence. (The prisoners were deemed to have begun their sentences at Nuremberg on the day they were imposed.) Raeder was released on 26 September of the following year, on grounds of his advanced age and ill health, having served ten years of his life sentence.

Dönitz completed his ten-year sentence on 1 October 1956. Neurath had died at his home a few weeks earlier. In May 1957, Funk walked out of Spandau, released on similar grounds to Raeder. He had served ten and a half years of his life sentence. Prisoners 2, 3, 4 and 6 were gone, and those remaining became increasingly hopeful of their own freedom. Spandau was now maintained for three men – Hess, von Schirach and Speer.

By the end of 1960, Funk and Raeder had died at their homes, and a few months later, the campaign for the release of the remaining prisoners, which was backed by Chancellor Adenauer among others, suffered a setback when Adolf Eichmann went on trial in Jerusalem. Renewed world focus on Nazi atrocities temporarily destroyed any sympathy with appeals for clemency. Nevertheless, petitions continued to be made on behalf of prisoners 1, 5 and 7, to the Soviet Premier Khrushchev; to Queen Elizabeth II; to Willi Brandt, Mayor of Berlin; to President Lyndon Johnson and President de Gaulle – all to no avail.

Von Schirach and Speer served their full terms of imprisonment to the day, and were released from Spandau on 1 October 1966. A large crowd had gathered outside to see them depart. Schirach was half blind, having been operated on unsuccessfully for a detached retina in his right eye.

The prison had now become a unique hellhole for one

man, prisoner no. 7, the seventy-two-year-old Rudolf Hess. 'I hardly think', he had remarked to his lawyer a couple of years earlier, 'I shall be kept alone in the most expensive prison in the world.' It was another of Hess's frequent misjudgements. The Russians had consistently refused to entertain pleas for his release, despite pressure from Britain and America, and they were not about to change their minds. If they had had their way, Hess would have been hanged at Nuremberg.

In May 1941, Hess had made an extraordinary solo flight to Scotland to try to secure a peace agreement between Britain and Germany. It seems he had been told by his astrologer that the stars ordained that he was destined to bring about peace. He announced to his British interviewers, however, that negotiations could only commence if Churchill were sacked, since the Führer could not be expected to have dealings with him. When Hitler was given the news, the Führer was furious. He thought Hess must have gone out of his mind, and appointed Bormann as his new deputy, ordering that Hess was to be shot if he returned to Germany. But if Hess had succeeded in his crazy mission, it would have left Hitler free to throw all his forces against the Soviet Union, so Hess's action did not endear him to Stalin and his successors.

Hess was always the most troublesome of the Spandau prisoners. By his own admission, he feigned physical illnesses and loss of memory, and he was always intent on drawing attention to himself. But he had genuine periods of paranoia and acute depression. He had made a half-hearted attempt at suicide whilst under detention in Britain. In Spandau, he made a feeble attempt to cut his wrist using a lens from his spectacles. The wound was stitched without anaesthetic, and Hess's glass lenses were replaced with plastic ones.

Now alone, Hess suddenly asked for a visit from his wife and son, neither of whom he had seen for twenty-eight years. He had last seen his son, now a man of thirty-two, when he was a four-year-old child. The boy had been named after Hitler's favourite dog. Ilse and Wolf Hess were allowed a half-hour visit on Boxing Day 1969.

In August 1974, Baldur von Schirach died. Apart from Hess, only Speer and Dönitz of the original Spandau seven now remained alive. The international movement for Hess's release on humanitarian grounds gathered momentum, but there was no wavering in the Soviet Union, where life imprisonment meant exactly what it said. The British, US and French governments were in favour of letting Hess go and closing a chapter of history, but they could not renege on their international agreement with the USSR. Hess had now become a moral and economic embarrassment. Whereas the western Allies regarded him as a 'frail old man', as the British Foreign Secretary David Owen described him in 1978, the Kremlin persisted in seeing him as a symbol of Nazism, and a possible rallying figure for German neo-Nazis if he were to be released.

There was some justification for the Soviet view. Hess had never shown any sign of repentance for his part in the establishment of Nazi Germany and its aggression. The disciple who had taken down *Mein Kampf* at Hitler's dictation remained fanatically loyal to his master's memory throughout his years in prison, and sometimes entertained delusions that he might yet become the new Führer. He was living in luxury in Spandau compared with the lives of a great many of the Russian people.

Rumours grew that the prisoner of Spandau was mad. But he was constantly being interviewed by psychiatrists who, though sometimes puzzled by his apparent losses of memory, generally concluded that he was sane. He discussed with the then commandant of the American garrison at Spandau, Colonel Eugene Bird, details of the

Vietnam war, the American moon landing, the British general election in which Harold Wilson was ousted as Prime Minister by Edward Heath, and the award of the Nobel Peace Prize to Willi Brandt.

Hugh Thomas, an army surgeon attached to the British Military Hospital in Berlin, came to the conclusion that the man held in Spandau was not Hess at all. Hess's medical records mentioned bullet wounds received in the First World War, which Mr Thomas could not trace. Hess was supposed to have been shot through his left lung in 1917, and even after all these years such a wound would, Mr Thomas asserted, have left its marks. Elaborate theories began to be constructed around the possibility that the real Hess had been cleverly substituted in Spandau by a look-alike. Frau Hess scoffed at this absurd idea. The truth is more likely to be that Hess never was shot during the First World War. He was a hypochondriac and a malingerer, and his records might well have been doctored later. Moreover, it has been argued by other experts that such a wound *could* have healed completely.

In 1971, according to Colonel Bird, Hess told him: 'The doctor has told me that I should have a heating pad in my bed. As you know, the electricity socket in my cell has been disconnected to prevent suicide attempts. But that is silly. I have a glass in my cell and if I wished to commit suicide I could smash it and use that. But I am past that stage now. I would not commit suicide.' In February 1977, Hess attempted to cut his wrists with a knife, but was caught in the act by warders.

At the beginning of September 1981, Albert Speer died in London. Hess was now the only survivor of the Spandau seven, Dönitz having died the previous year. The solitary confinement of the aged prisoner of Spandau had been made a little easier to bear by allowing him a small suite of rooms with his own library, gramophone records and colour television set. The cost of running

Spandau was estimated at around £140,000 a day by this time, most of the cost being borne by West Berlin.

On 17 August 1987, Hess was found dead. He had evidently strangled himself with a length of electrical flex in the garden summer house which had been put up specially for his use. The flex was suspended from a window-latch. The suicide occurred during one of the American months in charge. Hess was ninety-three years old. He had been in captivity for half his life – forty-six years; in Spandau for forty-one of them; and had been the only prisoner there for the last twenty-one years.

Hess's family believed that a ninety-three-year-old man would not have had the strength to strangle himself, but this has been disproved. Hugh Thomas now flew another sensational kite. Hess did not commit suicide, he argued, but was brutally murdered. In view of Mr Thomas's earlier belief that the prisoner in Spandau was not really Hess at all, this proposition seemed to be in the nature of a tactical U-turn in order to exploit the world's interest in, and speculation about, the last of the leading Nazis. What is clearly true, however, is that the earlier precautions in the constant guarding of the prisoners in Spandau had by this time been relaxed too far.

Within a matter of weeks after the death of Rudolf Hess, Spandau gaol was completely demolished, in order to ensure that it did not become a focal point for German neo-Nazis. A supermarket was built on the site, for British servicemen and their families in Berlin. Tea bags and rice krispies would not be the symbols a new age of German fascism could be built on.

10

The Maze, Belfast

One of the newest prisons in the United Kingdom, 'the Maze' became notorious as soon as it was opened, its name almost immediately as familiar throughout the British Isles as places in Belfast, such as Andersonstown and Ardoyne, Falls Road and Shankill Road, which few people on the other side of the Irish Sea had ever heard of before.

The Maze prison was preceded by Long Kesh, a former air force base between Lisburn and Lurgan in County Antrim, to the south-west of Belfast. It was like a prisoner-of-war camp, with Nissen huts in an enclosed compound, guarded by gun towers. It came to public notice towards the end of 1971. As the Provisional Irish Republican Army, which had commenced its new campaign of violence two years before, established 'no-go areas' in Belfast and Londonderry, there was increasing pressure on the Northern Ireland Prime Minister, Brian Faulkner, who was already seen by Catholics as a hardliner, to implement tougher security measures. On 9 August 1971, internment without trial was introduced under the Special Powers Act, and more than three hundred and forty Catholic suspects were arrested.

As well as widespread protests and demonstrations, there was an escalation of violence. Of one hundred and seventy-three people killed in Ulster during 1971, one hundred and forty-three were killed in the last five months, i.e. after the introduction of internment. There were allegations of brutality by the Royal Ulster Constabulary and the British Army against detainees, during interrogation in the course of the implementation of internment, and it was officially confirmed later that a certain amount of ill-treatment *had* occurred. (The European Court of Human Rights found in 1978 that some prisoners in 1971 had been subjected to cruel, inhuman and degrading treatment, but allegations of torture were not upheld.)

Long Kesh was divided into Catholic and Protestant compounds, and prisoners were allowed to run their own affairs to a large extent. It became a sort of terrorist training camp, where inmates were given lectures on revolutionary politics and guerrilla warfare in preparation for their later activities. There were several escape attempts, the most favoured method being the digging of tunnels under the fence. The Nissen huts were searched thoroughly at irregular intervals, and if tunnels were found, they were filled in.

In March 1972, the Conservative government of Edward Heath prorogued Stormont and imposed direct government from Whitehall, a draconian law enforcement policy being administered by the new Secretary of State for Northern Ireland, William Whitelaw. Meanwhile, a new purpose-built maximum security prison for terrorists was under rapid construction alongside the existing compound.

Her Majesty's Prison, Maze, was ready for occupation by 1974. It was claimed by the government to be the most up-to-date and luxurious prison in western Europe. It consisted of eight 'H-blocks', so-called from their shape in plan, each containing one hundred cells in the 'wings', the horizontal bar of the H accommodating offices, stores, medical treatment rooms, etc. Each wing of twenty-five cells had its own dining room, exercise yard and 'hobbies room'. The blocks cost around a million pounds each, but were built so hastily that there were constructional faults such as ill-fitting cell doors. The prison covered a hundred and thirty-three acres of land, and was surrounded by a high wall surmounted by barbed wire, guarded by water-towers and guard-dogs. The prison was for both men and women, Loyalist and Republican terrorists, who were separated but within earshot of one another, Republicans generally outnumbering Loyalists by two to one. The majority of prisoners were in for 'life', for murder. On 6 November 1974 thirty-three Republican prisoners escaped, though all except one were captured the same day.

The change of name of the prison from Long Kesh to the Maze was purely cosmetic, like changing the name of the controversial Windscale nuclear plant in Cumbria to Sellafield. The new prison continued to be known as Long Kesh to the inmates. As in the old compounds, they were permitted to run their own affairs to some degree. Whereas most of the prisons discussed in this book were hellholes because the authorities made them so, the Maze became a hellhole mainly through the activities of the prisoners themselves, who called the H-blocks 'hell blocks'. Both Republican and Loyalist prisoners organised themselves on military lines, with a commanding officer and so on, but the Republicans regarded 'the Kesh' as a political prison. The British government's flat refusal to treat them as political prisoners led to a long and bitter campaign which began with Republican prisoners refusing to wear prison uniform. By 1976, two hundred men and women were 'on the blanket' – covering themselves only with prison blankets and refusing to put on the clothes issued to them.

In 1978, the so-called 'dirty protest' brought the Maze to the notice of the world's press as well as to the European Court of Human Rights. It began on 13 March and took the form of a 'no wash, no toilet' campaign against conditions in the prison. Republican prisoners refused to leave their cells to 'slop out', alleging that they were liable to be beaten up by warders whilst they were using the washrooms. They took to throwing the contents of their chamber pots out through windows and spy-holes. Sometimes warders threw the refuse back into the cells. So the prisoners began pouring urine through cracks and smeared the walls of their cells with their excrement, and as the warders refused to clean cells whilst prisoners were in them, the cells were soon like sewage tanks. They became infested with maggots.

Prison officers had become official targets for the IRA and by January 1980, eighteen had been murdered, including one woman and an assistant governor. By the end of that year, there were three hundred and forty-one Republican prisoners on the 'dirty protest', which had also been taken up by women Republican prisoners in Armagh Prison. The Primate of All Ireland, Cardinal Tomas O Fiaich, had likened the conditions in the Maze to the homeless living in sewers in the slums of Calcutta. The British government remained unmoved, backed by the European Convention on Human Rights, which ruled that there were no grounds in international law for the claim to political status, and that the conditions under which the prisoners were living were self-inflicted.

Some prisoners had meanwhile escalated their protest into a hunger strike. The first seven such strikers included one person from each of the six counties of Northern Ireland. Their demands included the right to wear their own clothes, the right to refuse prison work, to be granted free association with one another, and to be allowed to receive one parcel a week from outside. Fasts as a method of protest had an honourable pedigree among the Irish, and the prisoners were encouraged by the British government's capitulation in September 1980 to Gwynfor Evans, the president of Plaid Cymru, who had threatened a hunger strike to the death if the government failed to honour its manifesto pledge to provide a Welsh-language service on Channel 4 television. The Irish demands were flatly refused, however, and on 18 December the hunger strike was called off. One Provisional IRA prisoner was critically ill. The

Revd Ian Paisley remarked provocatively that the failure of the hunger strike had made the Republican prisoners look 'mighty small'.

On 1 March 1981, a new hunger strike protest was begun when a Provisional IRA prisoner, Bobby Sands, refused food, demanding political status for convicted terrorists. Sands, whose twenty-seventh birthday came on the ninth day of his protest, was the Republican 'commanding officer' inside the Maze. Gerry Adams, vice-president of Sinn Fein, suggested a propaganda tactic of putting Sands up for a forthcoming by-election, and Bernadette McAliskey was his official proposer as Anti-H-Block candidate for Fermanagh and South Tyrone. Communication between the prisoners and those outside, on this as on other matters, was maintained by the common practice of smuggling messages, often carried in and out of the Maze by women visitors, who hid them in their underwear, or in their vaginas, wrapped in clingfilm. Prisoners would write lengthy detailed letters, or 'comms', on cigarette papers or toilet paper, and conceal them from warders by inserting them in their rectums. Smuggling messages and other objects in this way was not painful, one former prisoner explained, but 'you do bleed all the time and sometimes pieces of flesh come off. Everyone has piles'.

The communications were full of well-understood code-names. Sands was 'Marcella'; Adams was 'Brownie'; the prison doctor was 'Mengele' and the prison chaplain 'Index'; Charles Haughey, Prime Minister of the Irish Republic, was 'Amadon', and Margaret Thatcher, Prime Minister of the United Kingdom, was 'Tinknickers'. By such devices Sinn Fein was kept fully informed of everything that was happening in the prison during the 'dirty protest' and the hunger strike.

There were consistent allegations of ill-treatment and brutality by the 'screws'. It was said that warders would use the same fingers to explore prisoners' mouths for hidden objects as they had just used for searching their rectums. Prisoners reported being punched, kicked and dragged along by their hair. One man was said to have been held down by warders while another squeezed his testicles until he became unconscious. One prisoner was operated on in Belfast City Hospital to replace a testicle in his scrotum after being kicked.

On 23 March, Sands was transferred to the prison hospital. By the end of the month, he had lost eleven kilograms in weight. On 9 April, notwithstanding his situation, he was elected Member of Parliament, getting more than fifty thousand votes. Within a month, he was dead. He had become blind by the end of April, and lapsed into a coma a few days later. He died on 5th May after refusing food for sixty-six days. There was wide-spread rioting in Ireland – especially in Belfast, London-derry and Dublin. Other prisoners had joined the protest, and the second of them, Frank Hughes, died a week after Sands. The third and fourth to lose their lives were Patsy O'Hara and Raymond McCreesh. As each one died, he was replaced by a new hunger-striker in a relentless procession of self-sacrifice.

The British government said the deaths were cases of suicide. But Cardinal O Fiaich said that the men preferred to face death rather than 'submit to being classed as criminals. Anyone with the least knowledge of Irish history knows how deeply rooted this attitude is in our country's past'. William Butler Yeats had long ago given eloquent expression to this desperate philosophy in 'The King's Threshold':

> He has chosen death:
> Refusing to eat or drink, that he may bring
> Disgrace upon me; for there is a custom,
> An old and foolish custom, that if a man
> Be wronged, or think that he is wronged, and starve
> Upon another's threshold till he die,
> The Common People, for all time to come,

> Will raise a heavy cry against that threshold,
> Even though it be the King's.

Six more Republican prisoners lost their lives whilst negotiations were going on to try and find a mutually acceptable solution to the problem. Dr David Owen visited the hunger-strikers in the prison hospital and appealed to them to give the new Northern Ireland Secretary, James Prior, a chance to settle the dispute. On 3 October, after two hundred and seventeen days, the hunger strike was called off.

The British media called the ending of the strike a victory for the intransigent Margaret Thatcher and her government. But there was no victory for anyone in this depressing affair. The long campaign had taken its toll of prison officers as well as inmates. Besides the eighteen officers murdered, twelve had committed suicide. Three days later, James Prior announced that all prisoners in the Maze, both Republicans and Loyalists, would henceforth be allowed to wear their own clothes, and the other demands were also met, but there was no recognition of political status for the Republican prisoners.

The Maze prison's sensations were not over yet, however. On 25 September 1983, thirty-eight Republican prisoners in Block H-7 escaped. It was the biggest gaol-break in United Kingdom history. Ten of the escapees were still at large after five years. Two were recaptured in the USA in June 1992, including one who had been sentenced to life imprisonment for the murder of the deputy governor.

The regime has relaxed somewhat since then, though the Maze continues as a maximum security prison populated largely by men serving life sentences. Visitors are allowed once a week, though both prisoners and visitors are searched thoroughly before access, and prisoners who have served at least thirteen years are allowed out for a few days on trust during the summer and at Christmas. No one has – at the time of writing –

failed to return on time. The prisoners are well aware that just one defaulter will lose this welcome privilege for all his fellow-inmates as well as for himself.

Select Bibliography

W. E. Allison-Booth, *Devil's Island: Revelations of the French Penal Settlements in Guiana*, Putnam, 1931

Max Arthur (ed.), *Northern Ireland: Soldiers Talking*, Sidgwick & Jackson, 1987

A. Ash & J. E. Day, *Immortal Turpin*, Staples Press, 1948

John Aubrey, *Brief Lives*, Penguin Books, 1972

Brian Bailey, *Hangmen of England*, W. H. Allen, 1989

Noel Barber, *The Black Hole of Calcutta*, Collins, 1965

F. Beck and W. Godin, *Russian Purge and the Extraction of Confession*, Hurst & Blackett, 1951

Mary Benson, *Nelson Mandela*, Penguin Books, 1986

David Beresford, *Ten Men Dead*, Grafton Books, 1987

Eugene Bird, *The Loneliest Man in the World*, Secker & Warburg, 1974

Sir Norman Birkett (ed.), *The Newgate Calendar*, Folio Society, 1951

Edward Burman, *The Inquisition*, Aquarian Press, 1984

Michael Burns, *Dreyfus*, Chatto & Windus, 1992

E. H. Carr, *Dostoevsky*, Allen & Unwin, 1931

Benvenuto Cellini, *The Life of Benvenuto Cellini*, Heron Books, 1968

John Champness, *Lancaster Castle: A Brief History*, Lancashire County Books, 1993

Henri Charrière, *Papillon*, Hart-Davis, 1970

Anton Chekhov, *The Island: A Journey to Sakhalin*, Century, 1987

Marcus Clarke, *His Natural Life*, Penguin Books, 1970

William Cobbet, *Rural Rides*, Everyman's Library, 1973

Philip Collins, *Dickens and Crime*, Macmillan, 1962

Robert Conquest, *The Great Terror*, Macmillan, 1968

Tim Pat Coogan, *On the Blanket: The H Block Story*, Ward River Press, 1980

Alistair Cooke, *Talk About America*, Bodley Head, 1968

Frank Crowley (ed.), *A New History of Australia*, Heinemann, 1974

David Daiches & John Flower, *Literary Landscapes of the British Isles*, Paddington Press, 1979

Daniel Defoe, *A Tour Through the Whole Island of Great Britain*, Penguin Books, 1971

George Dendrickson & Frederick Thomas, *The Truth about Dartmoor*, Gollancz, 1954

Fyodor Dostoevsky, *The House of the Dead*, Everyman's Library, 1962

William Doyle, *The Oxford History of the French Revolution*, Oxford University Press, 1989

Charles Duff, *A New Handbook on Hanging*, Panther Books, 1956

Carolly Erickson, *Bloody Mary*, Dent, 1978

Robin Evans, *The fabrication of virtue: English prison architecture, 1750–1840*, Cambridge University Press, 1982

Lucien Fabre, *Joan of Arc*, Odhams Press, 1954

Jack Fishman, *Long Knives and Short Memories*, Souvenir Press, 1986

John Forster, *The Life of Charles Dickens* (2 vols.), Everyman's Library, 1969

Michael Foucault, *Discipline and Punish*, Allen Lane, 1977

George Fox, *Journal*, Everyman's Library, 1949

John Foxe, *Acts and Monuments*, Secker & Warburg, 1965

Julie Frederikse, *The Unbreakable Thread: Non-Racialsim in South Africa*, Zed Books, 1990

Thomas E. Gaddis, *Birdman of Alcatraz*, Gollancz, 1956

M. Dorothy George, *London Life in the Eighteenth Century*, Penguin Books, 1966

John Gerard, *The Autobiography of an Elizabethan*, Longman, 1951

Crispin Gill (ed.), *Dartmoor: A New Study*, David & Charles, 1970

Arthur Griffiths, *The Chronicles of Newgate*, Bracken Books, 1987

Fifty Years of Public Service, Cassell, 1905

Peter Hammond, *Royal Fortress*, HMSO, 1978

Frank Heaney & Gay Machado, *Inside the Walls of Alcatraz*, Bull Publishing (USA), 1987

Olwen Hedley, *Prisoners in the Tower*, Pitkin, 1972

Ronald Hingley, *The Russian Secret Police*, Hutchinson, 1970
A New Life of Anton Chekhov, Oxford University Press, 1976
Dostoyevsky, Elek, 1978

John Howard, *The State of the Prisons*, Everyman's Library, 1929

Pennethorne Hughes, *Witchcraft*, Longman, 1952

Robert Hughes, *The Fatal Shore*, Collins Harvill, 1987

H. Montgomery Hyde, *The Trials of Oscar Wilde*, William Hodge, 1948
Oscar Wilde: The Aftermath, Methuen, 1963

Michael Ignatieff, *A Just Measure of Pain*, Penguin Books, 1989

W. Branch Johnson, *The English Prison Hulks*, Phillimore, 1970

Paul Murray Kendall, *Richard the Third*, Allen & Unwin, 1955

Reg & Ron Kray, *Our Story*, Sidgwick & Jackson, 1988

Louis Kronenberger, *The Extraordinary Mr Wilkes*, Doubleday, 1974

Lewis E. Lawes, *Twenty Thousand Years in Sing Sing*, Constable, 1932

Philip Lindsay & Reg Groves, *The Peasants' Revolt*, Hutchinson, no date

Lord Macaulay, *Critical and Historical Essays*, Everyman's Library, 1907
History of England (4 vols.), Heron Books, 1967

Rene MacColl, *Roger Casement*, Hamish Hamilton, 1956

Frank McLynn, *Crime and Punishment in Eighteenth-century England*, Routledge, 1989

Robert K. Massie, *Nicholas and Alexandra*, Gollancz, 1968

Henry Mayhew & John Binny, *The Criminal Prisons of London*, Frank Cass, 1971

Terence Morris, *Crime and Criminal Justice since 1945*, Basil Blackwell, 1989

Terence and Pauline Morris, *Pentonville: A Sociological Study of an English Prison*, Routledge & Kegan Paul, 1963

Noel Mostert, *Frontiers*, Cape, 1992

Blair Niles, *Condemned to Devil's Island*, Cape, 1928
Edna Nixon, *Voltaire and the Calas Case*, Gollancz, 1961

Alexander Orlov, *The Secret History of Stalin's Crimes*, Jarrolds, 1954

Thomas Paine, *The Rights of Man*, Everyman's Library, 1915
Liam de Paor, *Unfinished Business*, Hutchinson, 1990
Nikolaus Pevsner et al., *The Buildings of England*, Penguin Books, 1951–74

A.J. Rhodes, *Dartmoor Prison*, Bodley Head, 1933
A.L. Rowse, *The Tower of London in the History of the Nation*, Weidenfeld & Nicolson, 1972
Andrew Rutherford, *Prisons and the Process of Justice*, Heinemann, 1984

Michael Scammell, *Solzhenitsyn*, Hutchinson, 1985
George Ryley Scott, *The History of Torture Throughout the Ages*, Torchstream Books, 1949
Martin Short, *Crime Inc.*, Thames Methuen, 1984
Richard F. Sparks, *Local Prisons: The Crisis in the English Penal System*, Heinemann, 1971
Amos O. Squire, *Sing Sing Doctor*, Rich & Cowan, 1935
Karlo Štajner, *Seven Thousand Days in Siberia*, Canongate, 1988
Z. Stypulkowski, *Invitation to Moscow*, Thames and Hudson, 1951

Hugh Thomas, *The Murder of Rudolf Hess*, Hodder & Stoughton, 1979
Hess – A Tale of Two Murders, Hodder & Stoughton, 1988
Harry Thompson, *The Man in the Iron Mask*, Weidenfeld & Nicolson, 1987
Basil Thomson, *The Story of Dartmoor Prison*, Heinemann, 1907
H. R. Trevor-Roper, *The European Witch-Craze of the 16th and 17th Centuries*, Penguin Books, 1969
Henri Troyat, *Chekhov*, Ballantine Books (USA), 1988
Tom Tullett, *Inside Dartmoor*, Frederick Muller, 1966

Sidney & Beatrice Webb, *English Prisons under Local Government*, privately printed, 1922
A. Weissberg, *Conspiracy of Silence*, Hamish Hamilton, 1952

Dick Whitefield (ed.), *The State of the Prisons – 200 Years On*, Routledge, 1991

Sabine Wichert, *Northern Ireland since 1945*, Longman, 1990

Greville Wynne, *The Man From Moscow*, Hutchinson, 1967

Report and Minutes of Evidence of the Commissioners appointed to enquire into the Condition and Treatment of the Prisoners confined in Leicester County Gaol and House of Correction, HMSO, 1854

Report of the Inquiry into Prison Escapes and Security, HMSO, 1966

Report of Her Majesty's Chief Inspector of Prisons, HMSO, 1984

INDEX